Nostalgia and Sexual Difference

Nostalgia And Sexual Difference

The Resistance to Contemporary Feminism

Janice Doane & Devon Hodges

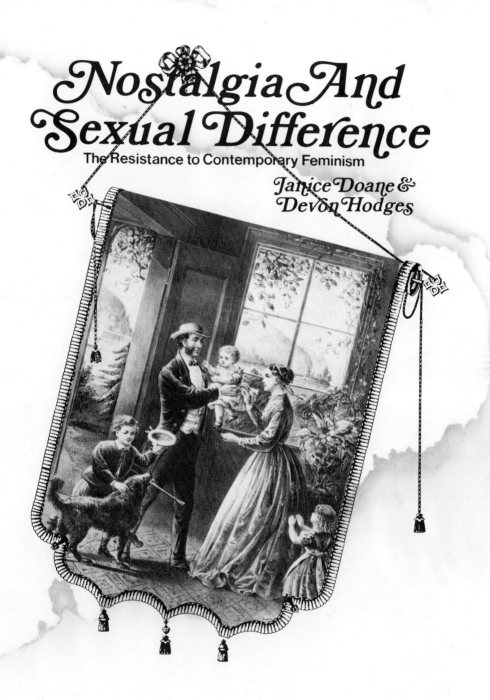

Methuen: New York and London

First published in 1987 by
Methuen, Inc.
29 West 35th Street, New York, New York 10001

Published in Great Britain by
Methuen & Co. Ltd.
11 New Fetter Lane, London EC4P 4EE

Library of Congress Cataloging-in-Publication Data

Doane, Janice.
   Nostalgia and sexual difference.

   Bibliography: p.
   Includes index.
   1. American fiction—20th century—History and
criticism.   2. Feminism and literature—United States.
3. American fiction—Men authors—History and criticism.
4. Misogyny in literature.   5. Feminists in literature.
6. Women in literature.   7. Sex role in literature.
8. Nostalgia in literature.   I. Hodges, Devon L.,
1950–   .   II. Title.
PS374.F45D6   1987   813'.54'09352042   86-28564
ISBN 0-416-01531-X
ISBN 0-416-01541-7 (pbk.)

British Library Cataloguing in Publication Data
Doane, Janice
   Nostalgia and sexual difference : the
   resistance to contemporary feminism.
   1. Feminism—United States—History—
   20th century   2. Feminism and literature
   —History—20th century
   I. Title   II. Hodges, Devon L.
   305.4'2'0973   HQ1154

   ISBN 0-416-01531-X
   ISBN 0-416-01541-7 Pbk

The authors wish to acknowledge Salmagundi and The Popular Press, in which
portions of this book have previously appeared.

*To
the future:
Cecily, Sara,
and Tristan*

Contents

Preface

ur book aims to show how poststructuralist theory can empower feminists by providing them with a way to analyze the strategies of representation. Interpretive strategies informed by poststructuralist theory have made it possible for us to conceptualize and discuss a frightening antifeminist impulse; we call it *nostalgic*.

Nostalgia, as we define it, is a retreat to the past in the face of what a number of writers—most of them male—perceive to be the degeneracy of American culture brought about by the rise of feminist authority. Without reading male writers, we could not have gauged the resistance to feminism. And we would not have known how feminist arguments about women's "difference" have been appropriated by antifeminist writers. Our work has thus led us to enter the current debate among feminists about the articulation of sexual difference: we question recent efforts in feminist writing to establish a unitary identity for "woman," "woman's sphere," or "woman's writing." At every turn, however, our work has been enriched by the very feminist authority that has so provoked nostalgic writers.

Our book is explicitly a collaborative effort. Not only is it co-authored but its existence has depended on the intelligence and support of many others. We are thankful to members of the Pembroke Seminar at Brown University, especially Joan Scott, Naomi Schor, and Elizabeth Weed for their friendship and critical acumen. We are also grateful to friends who read early drafts of the book: Steve Brown, Jan Cohn, Tania Modleski, and Bill Warner. The feminist literary theory group at St. Mary's College offered good advice about several chapters of the manuscript. In addition, two grants—Jan's fellowship from the Pembroke Center (1983–4) and Devon's research stipend from George Mason University (1985)—assisted our work.

We are also indebted to Ann Barr Snitow for her incisive comments about the manuscript. Her suggestions have made this a better book. For William Germano's generosity with both advice and support, we also owe a special debt of gratitude. Any errors that remain are, of course, our own responsibility.

While this book was being written, Tristan, Sara, and Cecily were born. Jim Mott and Eric Swanson assumed more than their share of the babysitting and so helped this book to completion. We greatly appreciate their practical and emotional support.

Introduction

ostalgia: *nostos:* the return home. Nostalgia permeates American politics and mass culture. While pulpits and podiums resound with the message that we need to restore American values and the American family, movies and television return us to the happy days of yore. This book explores a particular aspect of the contemporary effort to redeem an idealized past. As feminists, we argue that nostalgic writers construct their visions of a golden past to authenticate woman's traditional place and to challenge the outspoken feminist criticisms of it. *Nostalgia* is not just a sentiment but also a rhetorical practice. In the imaginative past of nostalgic writers, men were men, women were women, and reality was real. To retrieve "reality," an authentic language, and "natural" sexual identity, these writers fight the false, seductive images of a decadent culture that they believe are promoted by feminist writing. The battleground is representation itself: feminism is envisioned as a source of degenerate writing that threatens male authority. At issue are basic questions about the authority of women's writing and the power of male discourse to define reality.

Nostalgia informs the literature in many disciplines. To represent this diversity, we have chosen to discuss an eclectic group of writers. All those we analyze are influential in their own fields and often beyond. Each writer presents an indictment of contemporary culture that depends upon opposing the "deteriorating" values of the present to the "truer" values of the past, and each characterizes the "liberated" woman as implicated in this movement toward degeneracy. But nostalgic writers are not derogative to feminism in a simple way—on the contrary, they may even seem sympathetic toward feminism. The novelists we discuss—Thomas Berger, George Stade, Dan Greenburg, Ishmael Reed, and John Irving—share with many feminists a humanistic concern to move beyond stereotypic roles toward a more authentic "human" self; literary theorist Harold Bloom provides a model of literature that excludes women yet has been adopted by feminists to help construct a literary canon for women; and cultural critics Christopher Lasch, Ivan Illich, and Brigitte and Peter Berger make arguments that coincide with the arguments of conservative feminists. Nonetheless, an antifeminist impulse informs the nostalgic works of all of these writers. Each is anxiously provoked by the proliferation of feminist texts.

An early articulation of this anxiety is provided by George Gilder in *Sexual Suicide* (1973), his trend-setting treatise linking the decline of America and the rise of "Women's Liberation." Gilder, a sociologist who has taught at Harvard, is an influential theorist of the New Right. Disarmingly moderate in some of his attitudes, he insists in his preface that some of his best friends are feminists.[1] And nineteenth-century women might have approved his message: men are aggressive and uncivilized brutes; women by nature are gentle nurturers who perform the important task of taming men through marriage. But twentieth-century feminists have, according to Gilder, monopolized the media to promote the more dangerous proposition that sexual identity is not in fact natural. The opening sentence of *Sexual Suicide* immediately sets up a contrast between his serious text and the "liberationist" claptrap he believes is promoted in the popular media:

It is time to declare that sex is too important a subject to leave to the myopic crowd of happy hookers, Dr. Feelgoods, black

4

panthers, white rats, answer men, evangelical lesbians, sen-
suous psychiatrists, retired baseball players, pornographers,
dolphins, swinging priests, displaced revolutionaries, polymor-
phous perverts, and Playboy philosophers—all bouncing
around on waterbeds and typewriters and television talk shows,
making 'freedom' ring the cash registers of the revolution (1).

His first concrete evidence of this phenomenon is Phyllis Chesler's
Women and Madness, published in 1972, a book apparently providing
the hard proof that the media is in the business of promoting sexual
suicide: "A professor of psychology and a poet, [Chesler] believes
that American society is driving women crazy by sexist discrimination
and oppression. The only solution she offers is sexual suicide: the
abolition of biological differences between men and women" (3).
Gilder implies that threats to sexual difference are a direct result of
the control of discourse by liberationists in general, and in particular,
by women: "my chief preparation in writing this book was immersion
in feminist literature."[2]
At the typewriter and on television, women have made feminist
myths of sexual freedom seem as legitimate as what Gilder believes
to be the natural division between the sexes. He writes to restore a
truth blurred by unnatural and disfigured images: "It is a time when
few things are as they seem—and when appearances are propagated
everywhere. In no realm are things less as they seem to the media
. . . than in sex" (2). (Significantly, Gilder's book is soon to be reissued.[3]) Most of Gilder's fellow travellers—all headed back to the
past—write to wrest control of discourse from feminists. Robert
McCracken, for example, in a book called *The Fallacies of the Women's
Liberation Movement* (1972), explains that he writes because the
media—"flooded" by accounts sympathetic to the women's movement—provide inaccurate and misleading information about
sexuality.
A glance at the literature of the women's movement reveals a proliferation of heterogeneous texts the breadth of which indeed contributes to the instability of sexual identity that nostalgic writers so
deplore. In the sixties and early seventies, feminists literally rewrote
feminine identity; their texts tell women that they are not "naturally"
defined by their maternal capacities. But in that first charge of feminist
polemic there is no firm agreement either on what woman is if she
is not a mother or wife or on what she should do to realize her identity.

5

Betty Friedan explains that women need to work outside the home in order to develop a "firm" core of self (2). Ti-Grace Atkinson explains that women should focus not upon their personal identity as much as their status as members of an oppressed class.[4] Shulamith Firestone insists that technology will free women by freeing them from their role as mothers.[5] Kate Millett writes a blistering attack on the sexist characterization of women in novels, arguing that the image of women promoted by these novels imprisons them in powerless roles.[6] In the S.C.U.M. manifesto Valerie Solanis stridently announces that "Life in this society being, at best, an utter bore and no aspect of society being at all relevant to women, there remains to civic-minded, thrill-seeking females only to overthrow the government, eliminate the monetary system, institute complete automation, and destroy the male sex" (577).

The proliferating, unstable nature of the discourse about what woman is or should be is mirrored in the early history of the movement itself. In order to tell the story of the feminist movement, Ti-Grace Atkinson is led into the following labyrinth:

> In November, 1967, just outside Chicago, Women's Liberation held its first national conference. Radical Women in New York had already had a right-wing split off, W.I.T.C.H. These women in W.I.T.C.H. were not as feminist as those in Radical Women. After this conference Radical Women split up into separate groups, ostensibly to organize in more manageable numbers. But these divisions quickly assumed a political character. Several groups became 'study' groups. Redstockings emerged, temporarily as an action group. The most radical feminists came to the Feminists (98).

In this passage the words *women, radical,* and *feminist* gain and lose capitals with alarming rapidity as various groups attempt to capture these elusive signifiers. These early splits between feminist groups have proliferated even further; there is not now, nor has there been, a consensus among feminists about the identity or aims of the movement.

Anyone, male or female, might be made uneasy by the collection of differences to be found under the heading "feminism." What is feminism and what do women want? Even women who celebrate the heterogeneity of feminism want to embrace particular goals. But for men, the proliferation of different kinds of feminism is still more threatening—and not simply because of the overt hostility to men these writings often express, or because feminism provides a threat to privileges that are secured through male dominance. The many feminisms, the endlessly varying incarnations of the movement itself, make the concepts of male and female seem provisional cultural products, constantly subject to redefinition. The nostalgic writer wants natural, fixed sexual difference. Confronting the seemingly endless generation of feminist texts, his impulse is to seize upon some one aspect of the women's movement as its whole or true incarnation and then oppose this image to something he calls "nature."

Whether the feminist is fixed as the unisex militant, the career woman, or the cultural narcissist, she is a contemporary figure who is always opposed to what we will show is an equally contrived woman presumed to be a natural inhabitant of a better past. Let us give an example from George Stade's *Confessions of a Lady-Killer*, a book we will later discuss in depth. The protagonist describes the feminist villain Jude Karnofsky, "prize-winning authoress of *The Precedence of Women*, itinerant lecturess, talkshow personality, and cryptolesbian," as (if that were not enough) "poor, ugly, Jewish, and aggressive" (14). Unlike Jude, the protagonist's beautiful wife Samantha finally learns to enjoy her natural, prefeminist self: "She and the other women have been busy preserving meat and produce. . . . Samantha is becoming expert in many of the domestic crafts, about which she often writes in her weekly column for women . . ." (374).

Stade is well aware that his narrator's picture of the "feminist" is the one most exploited by the very media that Gilder so deplores. Samantha seems more natural than Jude: she is literally *in nature;* she is a mother, she is preoccupied by affairs of the private domain (a sex-segregated sphere that drastically limits the scope of her writing). She is also extremely content. More than that, she offers an emotionally appealing image to men who feel threatened by feminists. The image of Samantha harks back to an idealized past in which sexual differences were uncompromised by questions about the relation of these differences to ideology and culture. Stade understands the conventionality of this portrait—his protagonist is somewhat of a buffoon—but the authorial distance that allows for irony and burlesque is politically significant in so far as it protects the misogyny of his protagonist.

The nostalgic writers we analyze are not naive essentialists who believe that sexual difference is a simple truth existing outside of cultural codes. Unlike facile writers such as Gilder and McCracken, our subjects give language an explicit place in their arguments. Ivan Illich, for example, does not so much want to go back to nature as to cleanse language. He tinkers with linguistic constructs; his is a project of renaming that he hopes will bring the past back to us. Similarly, the Bergers understand that language is a political tool and that the *natural* is a culturally constructed category. But to replace the notion of the "natural," the Bergers substitute and validate the notion of the "objective given," a new term for those cultural products such as the nuclear family or familiar sexual differences that, for the Bergers, accrue value through time. The standard of validity is no longer nature but time, particularly the archaic past. As this example indicates, the crucial problem for such nostalgic writers is that in spite of their sophistication about language, they have a tremendous desire for a "natural" grounding principle, that is, a stable referent.

How does this desire for a referent work in the system of representation we call "nostalgic"? In a nostalgic mode of articulation, the referent plays a crucial role: it acts as an authentic origin or center from which to disparage the degenerate present and as the "truth" behind stereotypic sexual oppositions. It is always located in the past. At the same time, nostalgic writers know, with agonized awareness, that this past is a product of their own textual strategies.

Perhaps because of their doubts, nostalgic writers are defensively combative. They are fighting—many use metaphors of war—to protect their turf: a language whose power resides in its claim to bring reality directly before the eyes of the reader. Our critique of the strategies of these writers is obviously informed by Jacques Derrida's efforts to, as Christopher Norris has described it, "undo the idea . . . that reason can somehow dispense with language and arrive at a pure, self-authenticating truth . . ." (19). Even the most apparently transparent writing is dependent upon rhetoric, a rhetoric that carries with it the weight of truth and power. The most important strategy employed by the writers we discuss is to maintain a system of oppositions that is at the same time a system of dominance and subordination.[7]

For an example of how this strategy works, let us look at the opposition of *reality* and *image*. "Reality" can be supposed to be a secure and innocent referent because it, unlike the term "image," seems to stand outside of representation. But Derrida has shown that the terms of an opposition that seem independent of each other instead depend upon each other for meaning. In other words, the term "image,"

8

disparaged because of its association with representation, serves a crucial function: "image" produces "reality" and guarantees its importance by helping to disguise the way notions of "reality" depend on language just as notions of "image" do. Oppositions tend to operate on a hierarchical rather than equal basis: one term is degraded, the other exalted. Opposition is a power game. The opposition *male/female*, to give another example crucial to our analysis, is also typically hierarchical. The disparaged term, "female," helps preserve the value and integrity of the privileged term, "male." Those authors who want to maintain the reality of a distinct male identity need to keep the terms "male" and "female" separated and opposed. It is not always obvious that the "female" sphere is being disparaged, but when we see how *female* is placed in a system of opposition that aligns it with the degraded term of other oppositions, such as *image* (which is opposed to *reality*), *fiction* (which is opposed to *truth*), or *the present* (which is opposed to *the past*), we can see how male identity and formulations of the real are secured and their importance maintained by woman's traditional place and speech.

In nostalgic writing, the opposition *past/present* accumulates crucially important meanings. As we have seen, the term *past* is attached to other terms that make of it a locus of authenticity. So vivid does this constructed past become that the rhetorical strategies used to create it seem to disappear. Nostalgic writers are entrapped by the illusion that their strategy of opposition creates: their mythic pasts become real. They may be aware to some degree of the role representation plays in their stories of cultural decline. Yet the power of these writers is protected by their apparent ability to speak the truth, a capacity secured by the notion that language is transparent. In other words, self-reflexive writing, which calls attention to its own textual strategies, is dangerous to their authority. As Lasch notes, such writing "demolish[es] the reader's confidence in the author" (*Narcissism* 20). When nostalgic writers notice the workings of their own discourse they experience such moments of self-reflexivity as tortured conflict: is Lasch's past "myth" (fiction) or "memory" (truth)? His irresolution collapses the opposition between past and present, truth and fiction, he so ardently desires to maintain.

Nostalgic authors generally don't like modern forms of literature or modern institutions (contemporary culture exhibits a self-reflexivity that compromises a sense of the real). Feminists are implicated in this subversive modernity because they challenge belief in fixed sexual difference by exposing the strategies that are used to make sexual differences seem natural. More than that, they have been writing, writing, writing. And this writing not only challenges through its politics traditional ways of representing the "authentic" nature of men and women, but its very volume becomes a force that challenges male authority. Nostalgic writers not only want to put women in their place—they want writing in its place, too.

We have briefly suggested how the strategy of opposition can be used to legitimate male authority and disparage female authority. Our book will substantiate this claim. In Stade's novel, to give one more example, the narrator (a man steeped in the classics of a great, virile, literary tradition) takes murderous vengeance upon a whole group of feminist writers. Like Stade, who presents a "prize-winning authoress" as his villainess, all the writers we discuss try to tame women's writing and put it back in its place. Lasch aligns feminism with narcissistic, pathological, twentieth-century literature. Irving juxtaposes his hero's imaginary writing (that "feels so true") to the shapeless, timebound writing of Jenny Fields (that sells well but has the "literary merit of the Sears Roebuck catalog")—and this is just one of the ways that he attempts to defend and secure the power and prestige of male writing (13). Harold Bloom suggests that "the literature of Women's Liberation" has "contributed to our mutual sense of canonical standards undergoing a remarkable dimming, a fading into the light of common garishness" (MM 36). Ivan Illich, while relying heavily upon feminist scholarship, makes a point of opposing its weakness and dullness to his own superior insights. The Bergers snidely make feminist writing, particularly that which critiques sexist language, seem "demented" (50), and oppose this discourse to their own reasonableness and "plain English" (52).

The focus of our analysis is on the writing strategies of nostalgic writers and the way these writers engage the question of representation. American feminist critics have often focused on discrete aspects of representation; in particular, they have focused on images of women in literature. We also attend to images of women in our discussion of nostalgic writers: one question basic to our analysis is "How do these writers depict women and their writing?" Yet there are problems with this kind of analysis when description becomes entangled with prescription: attempts to describe a more "authentic" woman who is contrasted with a "false" image lead to the same old trap of articulating a "true" female identity and prescriptions for what "real" women ought to be like. Further, as we will demonstrate later, reversing traditional oppositions so that a "female reality" is opposed to "male images" does little to challenge a hierarchical arrangement of explanation and opposition designed to produce a privileged referent. Power relations are reversed, not questioned. Even novels that contain sympathetic female characters, as Irving's novel does, may still be oppressive to women. Characters are only one element within a larger textual system. As we will show in Chapters One and Three, narrative conventions themselves may operate to privilege male authority.

This brief defense of what we have chosen to do implies a concern about our own strategies, particularly our criticism of the methodologies of other feminists. More needs to be said. Feminist critics have always been concerned to put into question cultural constructions of *woman*. Yet the search for a way out of these constructions has led some of these critics to find some sort of reality—the real me, the essential matriarchal origin—both in order to counter false images and to provide something positive for women to identify with. From the early days of the movement, the feminist critique of traditional definitions and valuations of women left feminists themselves in a difficult position. If women were no longer to be defined against men, and did not want to identify with men, how could they generate a sense of self? The feminist critique of sexual roles in the late sixties and early seventies first negated the traditional notion of women's identity and then worked to develop a notion of an "authentic" self that was defined in relation to other oppressed women. Since the mid-seventies, an increasingly large group of feminists (they have been defined as "cultural feminists" in a fine article by Alice Echols) has begun to extol sexual difference in the hopes of modelling a feminist consciousness that will be subversive to a system that has long devalued women.[8] Ironically, in embracing a fixed, idealized sexual difference, these feminists share with nostalgic writers a desire to escape present oppression by attaching themselves to a stable referent.

The popularity of the work of such writers as Mary Daly, Carol Gilligan, and the new Germaine Greer is evidence of a strong interest in protecting differences in order to establish a distinct female identity both as an organizing principle and as an almost utopian alternative to male values and selfhood.[9] And certainly, in a time of enormous cultural change, the idea of an irreducible identity is particularly attractive. But we have yet to see how the promotion of fixed sexual differences—whether they are described as natural or culturally constructed—does anything but maintain an all too familiar system of oppositions and stereotypes. Since it fits so well the goals of an antifeminist male agenda, the assertion of fixed sexual difference by femininists is an extremely problematic gesture.[10] As Alice Echols sums it up: "Unfortunately, as recent feminism has become synonymous with the reclamation and establishment of a so-called female principle, it has come to reflect and reproduce dominant cultural assumptions about women" (440). In each of our chapters, then, we look not only at the strategies of nostalgic writers hostile to feminism, but also at the ways in which feminists who would and *have* criticized these writers are confused by their own desire to participate in the search for authenticity, a search that nostalgic writers are so passionately advocating and that offers only a traditional, stereotypic place for women. A place, not surprisingly, located in the past.

For this reason, our analysis of nostalgia distances itself from that early feminist criticism which exposed sexist images in order to champion a better "reality." We would instead advocate an awareness of how identity and reality are created within representation. As we show, through an analysis of nostalgic writers, the effort to get outside language from within language never works. On some level, these writers know this, too: the more self-conscious they are, the more hysterical they become. The characteristic tone that marks most of these works is a result of an attempt to violently fix distinctions— *past/present, reality/image, male/female*—that inevitably fails. In response to the subversiveness of language, nostalgic writers impose order only through conclusions that in different ways illustrate their own problems and desires.

Through our own text, we hope to encourage a different attitude towards the way *language* destabilizes *identity* and *reality*. Ours is an attitude of cautious optimism informed not by the advocacy of nihilistic relativity, but by the systematic critique of cultural codes that oppress women. That critique has made us optimistic in so far as the nostalgic writings we investigate demonstrate what a threat feminism is, no matter what interpretive strategies feminists employ. We are cautious because our critique also demonstrates that these nostalgic writers have nonetheless incorporated elements of feminist scholarship into their own oppressive discourse. The popularity of nostalgic texts and the power of these texts to appropriate dissident voices must be read as a massive effort to discredit and control feminist and other radical writing. Our book aims to subvert this oppressive effort. To do this, we have tried to remain sensitive both to the dangers of theories about the endless subversion of identity *and* the dangers of

12

theories that promote fixed sexual difference. As Biddy Martin says so well: "We cannot afford to refuse to take a political stance 'which pins us to our sex' for the sake of an abstract theoretical correctness, but we can refuse to be content with fixed identities or to universalize ourselves as revolutionary subjects. Our deconstructions are neither identical nor synchronous with those of the male avant-garde in spite of the very significant points of convergence in our interests" (16).[11]

Poststructuralist theories of language insist that no one can control discourse in any absolute way. But this limit on power does not mean that nostalgic writers cannot effectively challenge feminism or that feminists cannot respond effectively to their attack. Language reproduces power, sexual identity, and certain privileged referents; in very specific ways, nostalgic writing is involved in a struggle over who can speak, who should be allowed to formulate meaning. About this discourse we need to ask: how does nostalgic writing exercise its power? How does its language decide who should speak? Who has the power to assert what things should mean or how subjectivity should be defined? How can we resist the effects of such power?

Analyzing forms of resistance to existing power relations, Michel Foucault concludes: "Finally, all these present struggles revolve around the question: Who are we?" (212). Nostalgic writers feel the pressure to close this question. Yet their answers reveal how important it is to leave this question open. Even answers that seem flattering have too much power to control, define, fix into place.

Our analysis begins by examining one response to the question: "Who are feminists?" (The answer is: "Amazons.") In our opening discussion of four novels featuring the Amazon (written between 1973 and 1986), we begin to delineate how the nostalgic desire for fixed sexual difference works to protect the power of men's writing. Next we turn to Christopher Lasch's enormously popular *The Culture of Narcissism*—an example of a non-literary text that links a hostility to feminism to the promotion of traditional mimesis and the father's authority. In his book, Lasch reiterates the claims of a feminist critic, Ann Douglas, a sign that feminist themselves have told, and are telling, stories that preserve traditional forms of writing along with familiar notions of sexual spheres. Precisely because feminists have disagreed about how his novel should be read, our next chapter provides an analysis of John Irving's *The World According to Garp*. After debating some of the interpretive strategies employed by feminists, we go on to discuss the work of literary critic Harold Bloom. Bloom's influential theory of literary genealogy seems to exclude women, and as a result, feminist literary critics have argued that an alternate female literary tradition must be constructed. Again, we ask whether feminists ought to accept the notion that men and women have separate spheres of writing. As our discussion of Ivan Illich's *Gender* shows, the emphasis on separate spheres is found in other areas of women's studies and can be readily appropriated by male writers hostile to feminism. Finally, we discuss the conservative backlash against feminism as it is shaped by two well-known sociologists, Brigitte and Peter Berger, who have recently made a case for the importance of preserving both "plain English" and woman's place. Nostalgic writers locate that place in a past in which women "naturally" function in the home to provide a haven of stability that is linguistic as well as psychic: *nostos,* the return home. Feminists have long talked about woman's place in the home. We ask them to look at her place within discourse.

Chapter One

Monstrous Amazons

That night he dreamed that all of those giant Amazon women . . . were chasing him and the fellas through the streets. These giant women didn't seem to have much difficulty in catching them. . . . They were "monstropolous," as Zora Neale Hurston would say."

Reckless Eyeballing, *Ishmael Reed, p. 88*

 or the nostalgic writer, the impoverishment of contemporary culture is best described in sexual terms. Men have become effeminate; they have taken on the most despicable qualities associated with the stereotype of women; they are, in effect, castrated. The castrated man, indeed, becomes emblematic of society. America is "rudderless." One such writer, Robert McCracken, informs us:

It has been said that we live in an age in which there are no heroes. This is not true strictly speaking. We live in an age of anti-heroes. The male heroes . . . are small in stature, spectacled, high-voiced, incompetent, introverted, self-searching, frustrated, dependent, socially dominated, negativistic, and impotent. They bear a strange congruency to our society—once dynamic, but now rudderless, adrift on a sea of bureaucracy, indecision and liberal platitudes. The modern hero is as ineffective as he is effeminate. He stands for the abrogation of masculine values in this society; he is symbolic of the decline and fall of the power and prestige of the white male in America (141–42).

To explain how this disastrous set of circumstances arose, McCracken fixes blame upon feminists he represents as modern Amazons: those "slovenly, pants-wearing, combat-booted genetic females of the unisex species" (144). As he proceeds in his analysis of how wrong feminists are, of how they are contributing to the downfall of a once dynamic but now impotent culture, it becomes obvious that these modern Amazons are an enemy McCracken cannot do without. On the most obvious level, we can see that despite our sickly, effeminate culture, there is an exciting war going on, a war that encourages the expression of male heroics. McCracken's feminist Amazon suggests the unnatural, the hideous, and so her conquest functions as it always has: as a way to certify a male heroics that restores "natural" sexuality and cultural stability. Yet in the centuries of her representation in legend, literature, philosophy, and history, the figure of the Amazon has come to incorporate many rich and contradictory meanings and possibilities for sexual difference, power relations, and representation itself. She is a figure that has been embraced by feminists as well as their detractors. For these reasons, scrutinizing the figure of the Amazon becomes a particularly useful way of charting responses to feminism in the seventies and eighties. We propose to do so by focusing upon four novels that cover this span of time: Thomas Berger's *Regiment of Women* (1973), George Stade's *Confessions of a Lady-Killer* (1979), Dan Greenburg's *What Do Women Want?* (1982), and Ishmael Reed's *Reckless Eyeballing* (1986).

None of these novels is a literary masterpiece. The apparent "unworthiness" of these novels raises an obvious question: why do we take them seriously, especially when they are all deliberately comic? The first answer to this question is that we simply do not accept the division between popular and great novels as being as important as it is sometimes made out to be. Popular novels rely on the same narrative conventions that are operating in "masterpieces," and those we analyze here share their self-consciousness about form. Certainly the authors of the novels we discuss are writing books they hope will be commercially successful, but at the same time they distance themselves from commercial writing through strategies of irony and par ody. These strategies seemingly allow an author to rise above his commercial form while also making the reader who takes the novel seriously seem unable to understand a joke.

And standard wisdom has it that feminists are people who can't take a joke. (Greenburg even has his hero remind us of this commonplace: ". . . nobody has ever accused the [feminist] movement of having a sense of humor about itself" [48]). Our criticism of these popular novels may seem to be guilty of the same sin, but the humorlessness of feminists has something to tell us about the ideological placement of "fun" novels. The novels we discuss here are not nearly as playful as they pretend to be because, as we will demonstrate, they are confined by a discourse that promotes, often viciously, male prerogatives and power. Further, all these novels choose to have their fun at the expense of feminists—a politically significant choice. Stade, for example, has his narrator tell us on the first page of the novel that he is "the hero or villain of the narrative to follow, depending on whether you are a feminist or human being" (11). Neither alternative is really appealing: feminists are "inhuman," of course, but the novel's conception of the "human being" is itself based on stereotypic notions of sexuality. Stephen Heath nicely summarizes our concerns about the picture of sexuality and humanity offered by novels: the novel, he says, must "take responsibility . . . for the meanings and positions it adopts, and that responsibility cannot be avoided by appeals to the rights of comedy, satire, or whatever. There is no reason why, say, the woman's movement should be exempt from comedy and satire (and no evidence that internally it is) but comedy and satire are again made up at any time of particular forms which involve choices of meaning and position, of representation" (95).

Having said all this, let us seriously attend to the comic presentation of sexuality in these contemporary novels. In each, a rather wimpy, comically bungling man (of the anti-hero sort described by McCracken) becomes stronger, even heroic, in a battle with feminists who unmistakably incorporate the features of Amazons. Abby Wettan Kleinbaum, in her book *The War Against the Amazons*, delineates these features as they have accrued through centuries of Amazon lore. Describing how the Amazon has always functioned as an image of a "superlative female that men constructed to flatter themselves," she writes:

Although men never invoke the Amazon to praise women, they describe her as strong, competent, brave, fierce, and lovely—

and desirable too . . . she is therefore a suitable opponent for the most virile of heroes and a man who has never envisioned harming a woman can freely indulge in fantasies of murdering an Amazon (1).

The Amazon is the occasion of male heroics precisely because she articulates—in her unnatural and unrestrained sexuality— a challenge to the "right order of civilization" (2). Because "history wishes for the truth . . . and contains no monstrous element," the Roman historian Strabo excised the Amazon from his own historical accounts. To believe that the Amazon really existed, he tells us, would be the "same as saying that the men of those times were women, and the women were men" (qtd. in Kleinbaum 21). For the nineteenth-century writers Heinrich von Kleist and J. J. Bachofen, "the Amazon image stood for raw sexual energy which was the very antithesis of civilization" (222). In working out the evolution of the cultural stages of mankind, Bachofen claimed that "all the art and work of civilization could be accomplished only by overthrowing the extremely primitive Amazonian level" (Kleinbaum 221–22). Overcoming the Amazons, then, meant restoring civilization, a proper order that preserved "the basic relations between the sexes . . . [as] eternal verities of nature and everywhere unchanging" (40).

Preserving precisely this order between the sexes is the broad aim of Thomas Berger's *Regiment of Women*. In this dystopian novel, set in the twenty-first century, women have taken over completely. "The aspirations of the most extreme feminine militants," the book jacket tells us, "have finally been realized." Berger imagines that this can only mean social and environmental disaster. With Amazons in charge, urban decay, pollution, and inflation have become magnified into a monstrously oppressive environment. But most monstrous of all, men have literally become women, and women, men—the joke of a novel that purports to be a comical satire on contemporary sexual politics, specifically the desire for one sex to dominate the other. This desire produces ludicrous extremes of tyranny and submission: men and women are parodic incarnations of sexual stereotypes. In Berger's horrific future, however, it is the women who wear suits, smoke cigars, and wield dildoes to take advantage of the weaker sex. Men have become women, "painted, adorned, and mutilated" for oppressors who rape, goose, and degrade them (149). The novel, then, provides an obviously aggressive attack on the feminist project to envision and put into practice a better world. Berger's characters are so monstrous that they can only provoke nostalgia in readers for a return to a familiar order of things in which men are men, women are women.

The naive protagonist of the novel, Georgie Cornell, initially accepts his degraded position as an oppressed man, but in a stumbling way comes to the knowledge of more natural alternatives to the monstrosity of the novel's world. Significantly, this knowledge is not the result of a systematic critique gained by listening to assorted "male liberationists" but through the progress of individual experiences that force him to do some soul-searching about who he "really" is and how he acts. In Georgie Cornell and his female counterpart, Harriet, an anarchic individualism is opposed to a corrupt power system. Berger thus provides us with a familiar humanistic solution to oppression: the truth lies within the individual and in a resistance to extremes that are presumed to be always unfair and monstrous. Set against society, the isolated and unique individual is a source of authenticity. When the corruption of society has been satirically exposed, the authenticity of individual experience is the grounding principle to which Berger returns.

It is this humanist principle too that links Berger with certain feminist criticisms of contemporary society.[1] Feminists have argued, as does Berger, that sexual stereotypes distort the real selves of men and women, though women have suffered more than men from their imprisonment within degrading roles. The broad aim of much feminist research, and of Berger's novel, is to show how a corrupt power structure has masked the true identities of men and women by imposing bizarre roles upon them. *Regiment of Women* is meant to demonstrate how these roles are designed to polarize relations between men and women and thus deny their shared experience as human beings.

Berger and these feminists, then, seem to offer a critique of power and sex roles that will help to free us from a realm of misrepresentation that reinforces sexual difference. They share a belief, central to a humanist tradition, that one can move outside of power and representation to find a natural identity or "true" self. Both the author and humanist feminists want to appropriate for themselves, and presumably for all human beings, what has been described by one reviewer of *Regiment of*

Women as outlasting "all the forms that language and society attempt to impose on us" (Braudy). This shared assumption explains why a reviewer in *Ms.* magazine, Lore Dickstein, praises Berger's text: " . . . Berger is not arguing any one political line. His anarchist imagination exaggerates all sexual stereotypes into ludicrous postures, perhaps to show how they rob us of our freedom" (33–34).

Dickstein's hesitating qualifier "perhaps" points to an ambivalence that is evident elsewhere in her review. This ambivalence is produced by the tension between a humanistic impulse to celebrate an authentic self beyond the reach of politics, and a feminist commitment to a political position. Though she feels the necessity to warn feminists not to read the novel as antifeminist, there is in the warning a glancing acknowledgment of the novel's oppressiveness. The novel not only denigrates the women's liberation movement by caricaturing it as the inept, deceptive, self-serving "male liberation movement" but also subverts more modest feminist claims to be working for a better future. Dickstein, herself so much a part of a humanist tradition which celebrates the possibility of a self that is outside of representation and culture, cannot see that although the novel suggests the possibility of such a self, finally this possibility is not and cannot be realized.

Both Harriet and Georgie, good humanists, become increasingly aware of the monstrosity of their society and the men-women Amazons in charge of it. Though initially they are thoroughly brainwashed into an acceptance of their sexual roles, a number of circumstances and their own common sense force them into resisting these roles and confronting the Amazons, whom they overcome. They escape to "nature," represented by the wilderness of Maine, where their "natural" selves, formerly repressed beneath the grotesque and perverse sexual stereotypes of a corrupt society, begin to emerge.

But what sort of "anarchic" selves are revealed? Harriet begins to take a "natural" interest in cosmetics, women's clothing, and bearing children, and insists that Georgie take the initiative (literally that he take over the driver's seat in their escape vehicle), while Georgie, to the "horror" of his "socially brainwashed" self takes a natural interest in Harriet's breasts, feels himself sexually aroused by her, and finally becomes dominant. In other words, they have "escaped" back to totally familiar roles, which are validated in the novel by being based upon a true, biological nature. Anatomy literally being destiny, the privileged anatomical property, is, of course, the penis. The novel ends with Harriet and Georgie having intercourse (in the hope of having a child); Georgie, on top after a brief tussle, thinks to himself: "If he was going to be builder and killer, he could be boss once in a while. Also, he was the one with the protuberant organ" (349).

But the novel doesn't simply end by privileging the protuberant organ. *Regiment of Women* is structured by a phallic principle that informs the novel's crucial "joke," a simple reversal of who controls phallic power. In the novel's limited imaginative future, women in power will be just like men, sexuality will still be phallic, a matter of domination and submission. In other words, everything still revolves around the phallus, and Berger's stifling message is that everything always has and always will. His novel depicts a scenario in which women have wrested control of power, but the literary allusions at the beginning of each chapter tell a different story. Misogynistic quotations from Aristotle to Nietzsche tell us that women have suffered what men are suffering in the present of the novel. The quotations may suggest that women have cause to protest their degradation, but Berger's novel takes care to reinstate the owner of the protuberant organ in his position of power.

The universal truth of the phallus proffered by *Regiment of Women* masks the operation of cultural codes and strategies used to attain this truth, not the least of which is the humanistic impulse to award the author with a politically irresponsible position from which to speak. This impulse informs the confused commentary on Berger's novel, a commentary that has so difficult a time deciding whether the book is feminist or antifeminist. Berger also appeals to, and relies upon, a number of other conventions and codes: our expectation that we will discover truth at the end of a novel; our expectation that in the wilderness we will find freedom, itself a longstanding convention of the American novel. But primarily he manipulates our belief in the individual who can free her/himself of the corrupt power entanglements of society and its web of representations. *Regiment of Women* shows us why this belief is an inadequate basis from which to launch a feminist critique of sexual stereotypes. For Berger takes this supposedly anarchic, truer self, this purer individual, and simply makes him (and the reader who sympathizes with him) desire an old order of sexual difference. This desire, coming as it does from a "purer" individual, makes that order seem truer, more natural.

Regiment of Women demonstrates how power lies within discourse, in the manipulation of its codes and conventions, not outside of it. Consequently, what is often a salient issue in contemporary battles with Amazons is control over discourse, over the ability to give order, meaning, and shape to our lives. The new hero proves his virility not simply by conquering the Amazon, but by preserving male discourse. Berger's terms are set from the beginning: discourse is always phallic, so the question is simply who is going to control it. His Amazons are really men, but the traditional Amazon legend offers a more threatening possibility, the possibility of female sexuality and power that might in some way be radically different. What if the Amazons were attempting to promote women's discourse, a discourse that more radically puts into question the phallic order? It is precisely this possibility that George Stade's novel, *Confessions of a Lady-Killer*, addresses.

If the image of the Amazon both provokes and dispels male anxiety about women's power and sexuality, it serves a function analogous to that of another familiar female monster, the Medusa. In a brilliant article on the Medusa as a figure that, during the French Revolution, encapsulates political meanings as sexual ones, Neil Hertz discusses Freud's analysis of the figure as a symbol of castration—the Medusa as vagina, a place of hideous lack that turns to stone the man who glances at it. As Hertz points out, Freud sees how this symbol both provokes anxiety and offers a reassuring structuring of male fears—the penis is given multiple replacements in the Medusa's snaky hairs, her grim powers of petrification are translated, reassuringly, into the stiffening of an erection. But Hertz goes further by showing how the male writer he calls "hysterical" finds in the mythological female monster an image that threatens property and representation, an image politically dangerous, revolutionary. "Unnatural" systems threaten a natural legitimate order with its supposedly legitimate inequalities, sexual and political (Hertz 27–53).

Since both Medusa and Amazon operate as symbols that at once express and control male anxiety, it is significant that

George Stade's horrifying comedy, *Confessions of a Lady-Killer*, evokes both images. The cover of the book features a man in armor, a warrior who holds a sword (its sheath hangs down next to his protected penis) and, tucked under the other arm, the head of a Medusa. Because the man is not wearing a helmet, we can see that he has been turned to stone; his eyes, like a stone statue's, are blank. Blinded and petrified, he evokes the terrifying power of the Medusa's head he grasps. Though he has conquered his hideous enemy (his garb and pose suggest the battle is won), he has lost his potency in the process. Yet the Medusa, a female with an incoherent body, seems very much alive. We are left, then, with a question: does the novel redeem male selfhood and power or record its demise?

The image is still more complicated. Why is the petrified hero garbed in medieval costume? Does this dress indicate a nostalgia for a moment when virile warriors performed heroic feats for idealized women? The pun in the title of the novel on "lady-killer" suggests that the hero might be a courtly figure to whom women are irresistibly attracted. But the sword he brandishes has been used against a woman—the image thus defines male/female relations using a metaphor of war. We wonder, then, about the process one female character describes as changing the hero from "the champion of women" to a murderous, very literal, "lady-killer" (357).

The substitution of Medusa for Amazon involves a significant transformation. The Amazon is a figure of women's power; we should recall that Amazons were frequently imaged as fiercely autonomous mothers. Figured as the Medusa's head, the mother's displayed vagina becomes a hideous and threatening lack. Does the combination of the two figures suggest that what is at stake in the novel is not simply the fear of castration, but the need to control the mother's generative power? The power of the woman's organ is suggested by Stade's narrator himself: he is provoked into murderous vengeance by, among other things, feminist books and papers—"various organs (if that is the word) of Women's Liberation" (24).

In this respect, Catherine Gallagher makes an "obvious connecting link" between the fear of the woman's reproductive, generative power and the fear of the "semiotic behavior gone haywire" that Hertz points out but does not explain:

. . . if the mother is not properly constrained then semiotic riot is the result. One's name may mean nothing; one's property may have no natural relationship to one's name. One's self-representations may prove to be mere mental constructions . . . if one's mother was capable of the biological equivalent of system-making, of generating an illegitimate and unprecedented progeny. Thus, Tocqueville's fear of what Professor Hertz calls "the grotesque proliferation of theories" seems to me, not a fear of the weakness of the vagina, but a fear of its reproductive power (56).

Whether the vagina is the locus of male anxiety about women's lack or women's generative power (again, both fears rather irrationally operate in Stade's novel), *Confessions of a Lady-Killer* gives plenty of evidence of semiotic behavior gone haywire in response to the women's liberation movement. Our narrator, Victor Grant, is a little haywire himself—mad, murderous, and incapable (in ways we shall discuss) of constructing a coherent narrative. Stade takes as his satiric, and Victor as his murderous, target the whole editorial staff of the feminist publication, *Ms. Chief,* whose editor-in-chief, Judith Karnofsky is the best-selling feminist author of *The Precedence of Women.* Appropriately, the scene of Victor's first murder is a conference of the Organization of Social Scientists of America that features such feminist papers as "Deconstructing Gender," "Beyond Man: From Society to Sorority," and "Sexism and Stress: Gender Lag and the Androgynous Ideal on a Frontier Kibbutz."

In defense of his own practices, Victor's narrative is packed with allusions to the "great literature" of Western Civilization, from *The Iliad* through Elizabethan revenge tragedy (particularly *Hamlet*) to *Tarzan.* This arsenal of allusions is also important to him, he tells us, because it establishes his identity: "My reading is part of me. If you are not interested in the conclusions I have drawn from it, you are not interested in me" (26). Manager of the Columbia University Bookstore, graduate of the School of General Studies at Columbia, Victor reveals himself to have an inaccurate grasp of the reading that is supposed to establish him; he quotes for instance, the "great poet Wilbur Yates" and believes that George Meredith wrote *Middlemarch.* How are we to take Stade's irony? Obviously Victor is no master of the great literary tradition he uses to bolster him in his fight against the formulators of an emerging feminist discourse. Yet we have the feeling that there is a battle of equals going on here: as Victor puts it, quoting "the poet Wilbur Yates," there is an "attraction for superior men of whatever is most difficult among those things not impossible of achievement" (87). Victor, we understand, is not a superior man, but a rather pretentious, mediocre one; but those with whom he does battle—feminists—are not superior either. They are as pretentious and mediocre as he is. Only a mediocre man turned crazy would find worthy, if difficult, a battle with the formulators of feminist discourses.

Stade, then, establishes both his narrator and those he does battle with as crazy, letting the fun begin. Victor Grant's particular craziness is instigated by his passionate rage over the loss of his wife, Samantha, to Judith (Jude) Karnofsky. Jude has invited Samantha to attend consciousness raising sessions, and as a result, Samantha becomes dissatisfied with cooking "sunken quiches" and "grey stews" for Victor while listening attentively to his stories. Now she wants to delay having children and find a career. Victor impatiently cooperates with her "demands" but his simmering rage explodes when Jude convinces Samantha that the two of them must leave their husbands in order to find themselves and to devote their energies to *Ms. Chief*. Victor quits his job in order to begin training as "the avenger." It will take a real man to do the job, and Victor must transform himself from a skinny, chain-smoking wimp by jogging, consuming pounds of meat, playing basketball and drinking with other real men—those of the working class, "manly men who move objects for their living" and who are the "last besieged outpost against feminism" (268). Victor cannot rely upon his best friend, Jude's husband Bill, for help. Bill is not manly enough. A professor who drinks bourbon every night until he falls asleep, Bill submits to Jude's demand that he get a vasectomy. Worst of all, he stands helplessly by while Jude turns their son, Toby, into an androgyne. Victor, then, must avenge all humanity by rescuing Samantha, Toby, manhood, the male canon, and normal sexual relationships.

The objects of Victor's wrath and vengeance—the feminists on the editorial board of *Ms. Chief*—are horrifying to him because they both espouse androgyny and incarnate it. They are "menwomen," not real women and "bad imitations of men" (116). Victor describes his first two victims as hideously ugly, as monsters. Jude is "a short squat figure with kinky hair and flexed knees, handbag sweeping the floor . . . [a] lurching horror" (99). Stevie Dickenson (all the women have names which are ambiguously male or female), has a body that is "not an accident of nature but an assault on it" and is further described as "a scrawny boy" from head to waist and "a corpulent woman" from waist to foot (122). Erika von Plaack, Victor's last victim, is, unlike the others, beautiful and spirited, a woman who would have been a soldier if her gender had not prevented it. But she is the strongest manhater of the lot, and when Victor actually sees her having sex with another woman he knows he must kill her. All of his victims are either lesbians or flirt with the idea of lesbianism—Jude for political reasons; Stevie because she loves Samantha; Erika because, as she explains to Victor, "it was the most difficult thing I could think of doing among those things not impossible of achievement" (355). Erika, obviously, is Victor's worthiest opponent.

All the women Victor does battle with are androgynous, but they are not sexless. Their androgyny, in fact, serves as a reminder of "essential" male and female characteristics even as it appears to threaten such categories. Monstrous female androgynes demonstrate that normal women are supposed to be something else; but these androgynes also defuse the threat androgyny seems to pose to sexual difference by reproducing the male/female opposition androgyny is supposed to eliminate. Though androgyny has been adopted by some feminist critics as an alternative to familiar sexual oppositions, Stade's novel shows that androgyny insists on male and female characteristics even as it pretends to unite them. So, for example, Stevie is both skinny like a boy and fleshy like a woman, and Jude has a man's ambition for power but bears the mark of her femininity in her short stature and awkward feminine costumes. Androgyny may be Victor's target, but it also serves to make a case for the inevitability of sexual difference. Even Erika, who seems to transcend the limits of her sex, not so much as an androgyne but as a "supersexual" with Nietzschean powers of self-conquest and self-creation, is made equal to Victor, only to enhance sexual difference—her defeat proves masculine superiority. Here Stade most obviously relies on the construction of a "superlative female," an Amazon, to structure a defeat that will enhance the prowess of men. The Amazon Erika is also the exception that proves the rule; other women in the novel lack Erika's talents. Erika points to the "natural" place of men and women.

Significantly, Erika is killed by being impaled. In *Confessions of a Lady-Killer*, phallic power, the erect penis, and murder are connected, with the result that the assertion of male power seems both natural and cruelly pornographic. Indeed, each of the murders that Victor has so manfully trained for becomes a pornographic drama. With an almost constant erection, Victor stalks Jude for days at the OSSA conference, waiting for his opportunity to get her alone in her room. When Victor does manage to corner Jude, he presents her with a bouquet of flowers. She is dressed in a frilly nightgown; for a moment they find each other attractive. As the lady-killer's more murderous intentions become clear, Jude responds with karate chops and, when that proves ineffective, with seductive fondling. When her caresses turn into a tight squeeze on the testicles, Victor kills her by stuffing her mouth with fruit until she suffocates. In her death, Jude becomes grotesquely silent and, finally, truly feminine.

The love-hate nexus at the basis of these murders is echoed in other Amazon stories. As Kleinbaum points out, for example, Kleist's Amazon, Penthesilae, "after biting, indeed chewing the hero Achilles until he was lifeless, ruefully explained that her act was a mere 'slip of the tongue'; she accidentally 'kissed' Achilles to death" (222). Stade's novel, in which Victor is almost castrated during each act of murder, evokes the potentially dangerous loss of male power in intense love-hate encounters with women. Victor's next victim, Stevie Dickenson, also reduced to an attempt at seduction in her own self-defense, almost bites Victor's penis off. He stabs her to death. As Victor explains, woman must be (or pretend to be) submissive in order for man to maintain his potency, and the moment Victor's woman becomes aggressive, he goes limp; murder is his compensation.

Victor's murders have yet another pay-off. His victims are transformed. They become beautiful, feminine, human in their death. "Jude's body was purer, but also more mysterious, than her personality, which had left it. Her flesh was bright, but somehow hard to see, as though veiled in its own translucence . . . she had become entirely human . . . [I] restored Jude's femininity to her" (144–45). The dying Amazons, says Bachofen "represent fulfillment of true femimine subliminity, which is recognized only in motherhood and death" (qtd. in Kleinbaum, 35–36).

If female sexual energy and aggression is dangerous to male potency and authority, we can see why the submission of women, either as domesticated mothers or in their death, is essential to "true feminine subliminity." Victor's self-imposed task to restore "peace and order" must involve restoring marital harmony as a means of constraining and domesticating the mother. Jude is a failure as a mother; not only does she want Toby to be androgynous, but she refuses to stay home to take care of him. Samantha refuses to be a mother; part of Victor's conscious or unconscious strategy is to frighten her (as indeed he does, with Stevie's murder) into submission and back into his arms. But there are other examples of mothers in the book, women who are both good mothers and threatening in their power. Bill's mother, Miss Lilian, is a business tycoon who uses her vast resources to aid and abet Victor in his murders. She is a "real woman" who recognizes the worth of a "real man." But she has a little too much power; the end of the novel suggests that she too is about to be domesticated in a marriage to Victor's father. And Victor must do battle with yet another powerful mother—a huge mother pig at his father's farm, who goes on the rampage in order to protect her male piglets from castration. Victor proves his manhood by winning the battle against her, ironically, of course, depriving the little piglets of their manhood as an immediate result.

Indeed, all of Victor's murders have paradoxical effects. Victor hopes that killing Jude will be enough, but instead of immediately restoring peace, order, and Samantha to his arms, he only succeeds in unleashing more murderous vengeance, his own and others'. As in *Hamlet*, eight people are killed, including his best friend, Bill. And, by killing his last victim, Erika, Victor paradoxically kills a part of himself.

Victor's battle with Erika, his worthiest opponent, is also the most intensely sexual. Victor has fantasized about sex with Erika and is enraged when he spies on her having sex with others, a scene he describes in lurid detail. Erika is fascinating because she is his equal. While the police ineptly try to solve the murders of Jude and Stevie, Erika knows that Victor is responsible. Before they do battle with each other, they are intimate. Erika sits on his lap, rides around on his back, as the two tell each other things they had never told anyone before. Erika is more than his equal; she is his feminine double. He hates to kill her, but has no choice: it's him or her, male or female. Apologizing for the murder, both to himself and to the reader, Victor promises that if he has a daughter, he will name her Erika.

But if Victor re-creates Erika, it is within the safe confines of a marriage and narrative structure that ultimately restores marital harmony at the end. Victor, Toby, and Samantha escape to his father's isolated estate, Pinetop, which his manly father has made almost totally self-sufficient. The men hunt and build, and the women, including Samantha, who is pregnant with Victor's child, gossip about the men as they dry and prepare the venison the men have killed. Samantha loves domesticity and writes about it in articles for the local newspaper. Victor, still barely able to constrain the murderous sexual energy he has released in himself, fantasizes about "tracking down Bernadine Dohrn, Jane Alper, Kathy Boudine, Cathlyn Wilkerson, Susan Saxe, Katherine Power, Patricia Swinton, and the rest." But he realizes that he is "a son, a husband, a father, an heir, a man with responsibilities, with a position in the world . . . my time for adventure has passed forever" (378).

Victor's lack of constraint has generated his adventures, his narrative, but at the same time, this lack of constraint produces a narrative that is not fully coherent—either to himself, or the reader. At the end, Victor tells us, "I have gotten what I thought I wanted, almost" (378). Something is left out, left over, escapes and compromises the neat order he wants to impose at the end. Several reviewers have noted the "loose ends" in the telling of the story. "Who, after all, left the ice pick in Bill's chest?" asks John Leonard about the murder, never solved, of Victor's best friend. "And what has Richard M. Nixon, referred to persistently, to do with our [sic] fears of androgyny?" Mark Schechner notes that "dramatic continuity is not his strong suit . . . Because he writes with such astonishing ferocity, he can maintain a level of energy on sheer style, long after he's lost the thread of the story" (46). Clearly both Stade and his narrator are in touch with an uncontrollable anger, one that distorts and bursts through a narrative that is generated by this energy and yet must constrain it. Shechner accounts for the "ferocity" he observes in Stade's narrator by attributing it to Victor's "passion for social theory . . . nothing is more dangerous than a wounded theoretician" (46).

Schechner does not comment on the sexual fears that lie at the basis of Victor's social theories, theories that have to do, after all, with a woman's proper place, the place that Samantha is frightened of and forced into at the end. Ironically, the woman is domesticated within a structure—the nuclear family, the oedipal triangle—that simply reproduces the fear at the heart of Stade's novel, the fear of the powerful, even overwhelming mother. Within the oedipal situation, the male child must repudiate the mother, must separate from her in order to establish his own identity. If the father initiates this process with the threat of castration, the boy can accept his castrated status as temporary. Inevitably, he will be the father himself; he will inherit his father's property and place.

Several theorists of narrative have observed the ways in which the novel perfectly recapitulates this oedipal trajectory. We will discuss these theories in Chapter Three, but Stade's novel provides a good first demonstration of this principle of ordering. Victor's story of vengeance against women who threaten his male potency and identity is also the story of coming to terms with the father. "People tell me that I look more like my father every day. Everybody who works for him knows that sooner or later they will be dependent on my good will. They act accordingly" (377). This reconciliation with the father is not exactly a satisfactory closure—the violence it depends upon is too explicit. And there is a new twist: feminism is responsible for exacerbating the violence already implicit in the oedipal drama at the basis of the narrative of any male hero's life and adventures. With the rise of the feminist movement, the mother is less constrained, is given even more power than she normally has with which to threaten male identity. As a result, even more drastically violent measures must be taken to overcome her, or simply—as we see with Samantha—to frighten her into submission.

Stade is a self-conscious writer, but nostalgic for a type of male adventure story that can no longer be written. Through irony, he distances himself from the writer of that sort of story, Victor Grant, his narrator and misogynist *par excellence*. But how distant, precisely, is Stade? In his review, Mark Schechner claims that Stade's novel is a "tour de force" in which Stade "gets away with murder," because the point of this "comic exercise in social criticism" is that "ideas can send you off the deep end" (46–47). Schechner reserves a special place for the author, a realm above and somehow beyond the messy political scenarios he so vividly depicts. From this perspective, one could claim that the book is not really antifeminist, since Stade is simply revealing, through a protagonist he is superior to, the madness behind the misogynist insistence upon being a real man.

Yet Schechner does not discuss how feminists are blamed for the social scene Stade is satirizing. It is no accident that Stade uses a sexual metaphor to convey his critique of contemporary culture. In his literary criticism, Stade discusses his belief in the necessity of misogynistic energy for good writing. Appropriately, the male writer's relationship to his mother is always a crucial issue in this respect.

In a *Partisan Review* article commending Norman Mailer and Henry Miller, Stade reveals the same sort of ambivalence towards the mother evident in his novel. This article wierdly contradicts the analysis of Mailer and Miller undertaken in *Sexual Politics* by Kate Millett, who gratefully acknowledges Stade's help with her manuscript. Stade agrees that Miller is "hard to his women; he punishes them both for what they are, types of his mother, and what they are not, his mother." But finally, Henry Miller

showed Norman what it is like to be unburdened of the soft-
ening civility with which the women of American writers have
cursed their men. . . . Norman has been trying to show us how
to war with the mama's boy in oneself without losing either your
nerve or your mind. It is something one cannot learn from Hem-
ingway, alas. For these reasons Henry and Norman are right
now most inspirational protagonists—if you are a writer and a
man (619).

For Stade, the best in modernism is clearly that which severs us most
effectively from the "apron strings." It is not written by what he calls
"the Mama's-boys, [like] Proust, Joyce, and Mann (624)," who are
overly self-conscious, or those romantic modernists who "would
rather turn their anxieties in upon themselves than rule the roost"
("Romantic Anxiety" 500).

Confessions of a Lady-Killer pretentiously selects not Henry or Norman but Hamlet as its most inspirational protagonist. He is the pro-
totypical mama's boy turned revenger. (As Ernest Jones puts it, Hamlet's "difficulty was with his mother" [79].) By pointing repeatedly
to *Hamlet* as a model of his own text, Stade helps dignify male hysteria,
violence, and nostalgia for the good old days when the father was in
charge.

Dan Greenburg responds in a seemingly more amiable way to the
feminists' insistence that men take women's sexuality, desire, and
writing into account. Indeed, the title of his novel, *What Do Women
Want?*, promises us that women's demands are worthy enough to be
the subject of a good story. Greenburg, unlike Freud, will not throw
up his hands in despair over the answer to the question. His protagonist, Lance Lerner, has lots of answers, the most threatening of
which are "sovereignty" (270) and "I want to write . . . " Despite the
comedy and benevolent gestures toward feminism in the novel,
Greenburg reveals that something quite serious is at stake in this
typically '80's rewriting of the anxious story of men and their encounters with monstrous Amazons. Once again, we are given a vision
of women in power that graphically displays the myth of the feminist
as an Amazon whose sexual energy, aggression, and desire to write
is dangerous to male potency and discourse, and whose power is
ruinous to civilization.

In this novel, yet another bungling hero loses his wife to the feminist movement. Lerner believes that he loves his wife, Cathy, in-

tensely; she is "the male dream, the virgin whore . . . the smoldering temptress, petulant child, regal hostess, wide-eyed maiden, flaming bitch" and, last but not least, a substitute for his adoring Jewish mother, "a person with no needs . . . who lived only to serve him" (2–3). Lerner, as his last name implies, has a lot to learn; he must "grow up," recognize the immaturity of his attitudes toward women, discover what they want. He will be a better man for it in the end, and it is implied that feminists have something positive to contribute to this process. Cathy initiates this process by becoming "the last woman in Manhattan to embrace the feminist movement" (3). Tired of serving Lance's needs, and eager to discover who she really is, she moves out on him and begins to write a novel about her experiences.

When Lance stumbles back into the dating game, he discovers to his dismay that male/female relations have changed drastically in the eight years he's been married and out of circulation. During his marriage to Cathy, Lerner had always managed to "nip the peaks of her sexual passion because they made him uncomfortable. They made him feel he was losing control, and he was terrified of losing control" (5). The women he meets now are not so submissive; the new woman is sexually demanding and aggressive. Poor Lance is, in effect, raped in each of his encounters with women. Stevie, a policewoman, leaves Lance handcuffed, naked and spread-eagled, to the bed while she runs out to replenish the liquor supply. Gladys Oliphant, the building superintendent, finds the helpless Lance and has her way with him. Claire, the beautiful six-foot-tall wife of his publisher, requires Lance's sexual favors in exchange for getting Lance the business deal he wants on his latest book. Two beautiful Chinese teenagers keep house for him, but seduce him one day when he is sick and too weak to resist. Through it all, Lance protests that he is not in control, not responsible for these rapes and seductions. He protests until he learns to admit that he is responsible, that he not only enjoyed being raped and seduced, but welcomed it.

The not-so-subtle implication here is that women, too, want to be raped. Like Berger, Greenburg simply reverses the usual sexual hierarchy putting women on top and men on the bottom, so as to demonstrate that when it comes right down to it, women are just like men and want the same thing: "he had ultimately concluded that women wanted . . . romance, excitement, security, sovereignty, acknowledgment, unconditional love, money, a good fuck—everything, in short, that men wanted too" (372). This being the case, it follows that if a man can admit that he enjoys being passive, being raped, finds, indeed, that it is "liberating" (11), a woman must really enjoy it, too. Now that men are in a subservient position, they can tell us what it's like to be a woman, and how enjoyable it is to be dominated. This "truth" is further reinforced by the women's admissions in the novel. Despite her tough-girl act, Stevie admits she likes to be dominated. Gladys Oliphant had been raped, but it is depicted as one of the more exciting moments in her otherwise sexually frustrated life. And when a group of extremist feminists attempt to avenge the rape of a Puerto Rican woman, they are amazed by her downright hostile ingratitude.

In spite of his protestations to the contrary, Lance is always in control of the women he encounters and their unbounded sexual appetites. The keys to his success are his own virility and his status as a best-selling writer. Women are initially attracted to, and then become dependent upon, his sexual prowess. With the exception of Claire, every woman who seduces him does so because he is famous; they want his advice and they want to emulate his literary celebrity. Women's sexuality is unbounded; so too is their desire to write. Greenburg here satirizes a burgeoning literary marketplace that is beginning to accommodate the "second-rate" genres of the previously silent—blacks, Chinese, women: Gladys writes Barbara Cartland romances; Stevie writes about the celebrities she knows; Cathy writes about a woman discovering herself; the black writer, Ernest, writes about an oppressed life that made him turn to crime. None of these aspirations turns out to be a real threat to Lance, who endures as the important writer, while the others turn to activities more important to them. Stevie opens a restaurant for celebrities, while Ernest becomes a lawyer and politician. Cathy turns from writing novels to literary criticism, and Gladys becomes a best-selling writer of romances; but both are finally happiest because they are mothers to Lance's sons.

Once again, then, the primary issue in the novel is the control of women's generative power. Like Victor Grant, Lance must confront and control a number of threatening mothers. First, in his therapy sessions, he must confront his ambivalent attachment to and anger at his own mother, and realize that "making all women your mother was a way of avoiding growing up" (263). Greenburg, like Stade, recognizes the necessity of severing the apron strings; in the '80's the idea is clichéd psychobabble, which Greenburg nonetheless takes seriously. But in the grand finale of the novel Lance confronts even fiercer and more threatening mothers—undomesticated Amazons.

In his most exciting adventure on the road to maturity, Lance finds himself on a plane hijacked by crazed feminists. These androgynous women, "built like stevedores, uniformly short and stocky and very broad in the shoulders" (38), begin their careers as a group of movers called the Motherloaders. (Of course, they help move Lance's wife out.) In Stade's novel, Victor proclaims that the men who move around furniture are the last bastion of real manhood, but in the '80's even that bastion has been stormed. The leader of the Motherloaders, June Wedding (her name a commentary on the fact that she could never expect to have one) is, of course, writing a "bitter yet poetic first novel" (216). Bored by their moving jobs, and with a more ambitious writing project in mind (a book on rape), the Motherloaders transform themselves into a group called MATE (Men Are The Enemy), a group designed to castrate and abuse men they suspect of being rapists. When their feminist sisters do not show support for these activities, the members of MATE decide to hijack a plane to Mannihanni, an island where "women ruled and men were second class citizens" (247). As it turns out, none of the Motherloaders' transformations are really politically motivated. As June explains to Lance: "You do something that doesn't particularly interest you for a while, and then one day something better comes along" (332).

The mother who rules the island of Mannihanni, Momma Doc, is far more intimidating. She is "a grostesque parody of what [Lance] felt all women wanted" (356). What does she want? Power, sex, to write a book and go on the *Tonight Show*. But her sexual demands are particularly threatening because she decapitates those who have sex with her, after which the male body is eaten. Certainly this horrifying vision of woman's desire encourages the reader to want men back in charge. Lance must live up to his first name, must become the spear that conquers the Amazon.

His weapon, however, is not a spear, but words; once again he masters women because of his abilities as a writer. He sweet-talks Mamma Doc (every woman wants to be flattered) and promises to write her biography, a biography that will be so interesting it will get her on the *Tonight Show*. In return, Mamma Doc releases Lance and the other hijacked hostages, but Lance's favors to Mamma Doc don't stop once he gets home. With his help, Mamma Doc's country, which is in a shambles, becomes a modern nation. The Amazon has not only been overcome, she's been civilized.

This calls for celebration, and the novel ends in a feast of plenty. Everyone gets everything they could have ever wanted. Lance, our hero, gets Cathy back, and Cathy not only wants to come back but she gets what she really wants, a baby. Gladys, too, gets a baby—Lance's. Lance's Chinese lover, whom he introduces to Ernest, the black writer, also gets a baby, and Ernest gives up writing to become a successful politician. And so it goes. All the characters are in some way indebted to Lance's seed, his power and influence, for getting whatever they want. Who says that life under the father isn't good?

The novel, then, an extraordinary phallic fantasy, banishes the threatening and dangerous uncertainty posed by its title, the question of women's desire. What women want, we discover, is a man to protect and dominate them, a good fuck, children. Other answers simply lead to an intolerable monstrosity: sovereignty leads to Mamma Docs, revenge leads to the Motherloaders, independence leads to boredom (Lance's wife quickly tires of her newly found independence). But the worst possible answer, the one Greenburg writes his novel to foreclose, is that there is no answer, that feminine desire is uncontainable and that the "semiotic behavior gone haywire" that results from its expression might lead not to a reversal of sex roles but to the unmasterable proliferation of words.

Ishmael Reed's *Reckless Eyeballing* (1986) is a recent addition to this genre of nostalgic texts, for it too depends upon the image of the monstrous Amazon to express male anxieties about female authority. *Reckless Eyeballing* is another "comic" novel with serious intentions that features the adventures of a male writer and his confrontation with feminist writers. Like Stade's Victor Grant, Ian Ball, the protagonist, assaults feminist writers: he is the Flower Phantom who ties up black feminist writers and shaves their hair off. Like Greenburg's novel, *Reckless Eyeballing* is the story of a male writer's education: he apparently learns from feminists even as he first assaults them and then helps them return to their natural sphere, the home. At the end of the novel, Ian Ball returns home himself ("Come back to the way things used to be," reads the billboard about his birthplace, the Caribbean [119]) where the enigma of Ball's identity is resolved and we learn who his father really was.

Before he can return home, Ian must clash with his most powerful adversary, a white feminist named Becky French who is depicted as an Amazon: "Becky wore a P.O.W. haircut, khaki-colored blouse, and baggy pants" (46). Becky—and all white feminists—are dangerous in *Reckless Eyeballing* because they are in control of the publishing world, and through the power they wield can make or break black writers. To be successful Ian Ball, who is a black playwright, must pander to Becky and her feminist demands. But more insidiously, the novel also attempts to explain the recent success of black women writers in the same terms.

In this respect, Reed's novel can be read in the context of a debate about the recent popularity of black women writers, a popularity some would attribute to their negative portrayal of black men. Mel Watkins, writing in *The New York Times*, explains that at the present, when black women writers are more popular than black male writers, black male writers have asked: are black women writers more successful precisely because white audiences want to hear about "discord in the black community," especially about the brutal oppression of black women by black men? In an interview with Watkins, Reed contends, "It may all come down to sales, because it seems to me that the marketable element in many of those books is the attack on black men" (36). Reed's book is itself about the success of black women writers who vilify black men. But his novel explains the antagonism between black male and female writers by blaming it on the corrupting influence of white feminists. Because they are in control of the writing market itself (an extraordinary idea), white feminists have been able to seduce and corrupt black women writers, who are otherwise "naturally" loyal to black men. The novel calls for a reconciliation between black male and female writers: it ends with an image of a flag of truce.

Yet Reed can only grant this reconciliation on his own terms. It is women's authority, not just negative portraits of black men, that bothers Reed. Indeed, the debate about these images emphasizes only one aspect of black women's writing.[2] Like Berger, Stade, and Greenburg, Reed conflates the implications of Medusa and Amazon to suggest that successful feminist writers are "unnatural" monsters bent on castrating men. The reconciliation at the end of the novel depends on not only defeating the white feminist Amazon, Becky, but also on returning black women writers to *their* proper place and sexuality.

Reed's book opens with a dream image of feminists who threaten castration through the symbol of a snake (the Medusa's hair). And as the story unfolds, we learn that though women accuse men of "reckless eyeballing," women, like Medusa, are the ones with the dangerous stare. Ian Ball (whose name is meant to evoke "eyeball") has written a play called "Reckless Eyeballing." Its plot tells a "true story": " . . . this [white] vixen intrudes upon his [a black man's] space, glares at him with lust in her eyes, and when he pays no attention accuses him of reckless eyeballing, causing her husband and his friends to lynch the lad until he is dead" (103).[3] Here the cultural roles normally assigned to men and women—men look, women are looked at—are reversed. In Reed's book, as in the play Ian Ball wants to write, men are the victims and women the aggressors, particularly white feminists (who are connected with the Nazis), even though feminists like to believe that women are the ones who are oppressed. Reed takes his fantasy of women as victimizers to inordinate extremes. He has Tremonisha Smarts, his central black female character, declare that "statistics" show

> The women are the ones who are killing the men, and they get off too, as though there were some kind of bounty on black men. In my new play I tell the truth, and I know Becky and her friends will write me off after it's produced. It's about a woman who leaves her husband for another woman only to discover that she's a batterer. See, this is a problem that the male-loathing feminists don't want to discuss: women beating up on women. It's an epidemic, and the women's shelters are full of women who are fleeing other women.

If this quotation seems puzzling, it is because Tre's assertions provide an astounding reversal of the facts about battered women. Can Reed believe this? Are we supposed to doubt Tre in her moment of truth? Tre's declaration here, which is part of a larger confession about how wrong she has been, reveals that it is black feminist writers who "learn" the most in *Reckless Eyeballing*. Ian's success vindicates the truth of his perspective: besides fame, his play wins him the apologies of white feminists and the applause of those touchstones of reality, "ordinary black and white everyday people" (104). Ian Ball claims that he learns something from the black women he confronts and assaults: "Tre had taught him that there was more to a woman than a cunt. Much more" (120). Yet Reed's book in effect yields nothing more to them. Black women writers (Reed's narrator cannot even get some of their names right: "Paula Marshall" [128] "Toni Case Bambara" [119]) must come to understand that white feminists have seduced black women writers away from their true selves. These true selves are to be found in heterosexual relationships with men, not in friendships with women or the feminist movement. After a cat fight with her white feminist sponsor, Becky, (a fight in which Tre argues that Becky has become a man) Tre moves to Yuba City to get married, rehabilitate her junkie husband, and have babies. Even the black woman writer and Ian Ball's dangerously powerful mother, who have banded together at the end of the novel, simply talk about childbirth and the generative power of the father. Reed's message is quite clear: black women writers have been the servants of white feminists for too long. They have demeaned black men in the process, but mostly they have demeaned *themselves*, distorting and corrupting their natural feminine identity.

Ishmael Reed is an intelligent, experimental writer. Why does he resort to unconvincing realism in a book that, as a reviewer for the *New York Times* points out, "does a disservice to Mr. Reed's own notable career"? (Kakutani 12). The answer lies in his anxiety about the proliferation of feminist texts and the power of women's writing to dislocate the real by challenging "natural" sexual identity and thereby male authority. Again, the generative power of the mother is the problem. In Reed's novel, women's desire is explained as a desire for black men or simply a desire to be desirable. In a passage dripping with condescension, Ian Ball explains that non-white women are bitter not because of their marginality in a white and patriarchal society, but because they can't look like white women. Such explanations attempt to contain the threat of women's desires and sexuality.

For Berger, Stade, Greenburg, and Reed, women's desire and sexuality are increasingly posed as a threat to the realm of representation. Feminist writings are perceived as having been produced from "organs" of Women's Liberation, much as the vagina is capable of generating "illegitimate and unprecedented progeny." The question, then, for each of the writers we have discussed is how to control this reproductive capability.

One answer is to tame the threatening, extremely heterogeneous issue of women's desire by seizing on one image as its true incarnation—here, the image of the Amazon. Because this image has always carried connotations of women's power, dignity, autonomy, and "raw" sexuality, women writers from Christine de Pizan to contemporary feminist lesbians have adopted the Amazon story. But these women writers repress the ending of the story—the Amazon's conquest by the heroic male warrior—and emphasize the power of the Amazon to articulate women's power and a sexuality that is dangerous to a sexual politics in which men are on top. Nostalgic writers, of course, never leave any ending open. On the contrary, the ending of the story is what Berger, Stade, Greenburg, and Reed most celebrate: it is meant to provide the definitive answer to the threat of women's desire.

These books are both tedious and compelling. Tedious because Berger, Stade, Greenburg, and Reed tiresomely repeat each other in their insistence upon a "natural order" that simply replicates an entrenched and familiar order of sexual difference, an order that in these novels relies especially upon the most clichéd conventions of the American novel.[4] What lies "outside" of the monstrous culture ruled by Amazons is a "nature" occupied by stereotypes: hunter Georgie and his pregnant Harriet; hunter Victor and his pregnant Samantha; sword/pen brandisher Lance and his pregnant Cathy. In Reed's book a natural sexual identity is reasserted for the female writer in Yuba City, though the male protagonist does not get married himself. And, "naturally," we have an author who is also supposed to be outside all the cultural codes he is so obviously reproducing, despite the fact that these books, as even their authors must realize, are consumer products. They are meant to be consumed, not simply because they are written to be best-sellers but because they are compelling narratives, both prompting and relying upon what Walter Benjamin calls the reader's "consuming interest" or desire for the repose at the end of the novel, its resolution (101).

The resolution of these novels, which vanquish the Amazon in order to insist upon the naturalness of phallic discourse, male dominance, and female subordination, all refer back to a "past" that never was. As Abby Wettan Kleinbaum points out, at the beginning of written history, even in the work of Herodotus, we already have a tale of how man overcame the Amazon, restoring a proper order and guaranteeing the eternal truth of fixed sexual difference. In other words, to find that original proper order we must go back to a pretextual place *that does not exist*. In the novels we have read, this nostalgic return, reinforced by the tired conventions of male adventure stories, can barely find its justification by posing as an answer to the threat of a feminist enemy. In order to establish *themselves* as cultural heroes, nostalgic writers need that enemy more than they can admit.

Chapter
Two

Feminism
and the
Decline
of
America

*I*n a recent article entitled "The Politics of Nostalgia," Christopher Lasch takes up the cudgel of reality, as he has many times before, to flail the dangerous illusions of a degenerate modern culture. Skeptical of claims that we are "awash in nostalgia" (Politics 66), Lasch blames the media—that producer of false images—and the intellectuals; the former capitalize on the appeal of nostalgia, while the latter denounce nostalgia, the "ghosts" of the past, in order to salvage a specter of hope (65). If the media's exploitation of nostalgia is a form of sentimental escapism, then so too is the intellectuals' righteous debunking of it. According to Lasch, nostalgia idealizes the past, while those who denouce nostalgia simply want to ignore the importance of the past. Both groups avoid confrontation with the *real* past and its influence on the present. For Lasch, what gets lost in the debate about nostalgia is history itself. As his article's subtitle announces, we are "Losing history in the mists of ideology" (Politics 65).

As do Peter and Brigitte Berger, whose work we will discuss in detail later, Lasch opposes himself both to intellectuals and to "those who command the mass media" (Politics 70). Attacks on the "New Class" of knowledge producers and heartfelt claims to speak for ordinary people are expressions of a hostility to representation that unites neoconservatives like the Bergers and a radical traditionalist like Lasch.[1] Ordinary people, he tells us, are not really seduced by or appreciative of nostalgia. Instead, overwhelmed by the burden of their personal, ethical, and racial pasts, ordinary people go their beleaguered way, unable to avoid a reckoning with their real history. Because Lasch too is burdened by the past, he believes he stands outside both the nostalgia and anti-nostalgia camps. He enjoys a "realistic perception of decline" (Politics 68).[2]

Lasch defines nostalgia as sentimental feeling, a luxurious romanticism, and anti-nostalgia as an over-valuation of the present. Defining nostalgia as mere "feeling" allows him to avoid a discussion about how the past is inevitably a construct. For Lasch, the past is simply there, as an entity, a grounding principle. And since he believes he knows its truth, he believes he cannot be nostalgic. The implication is that we too could *see* this substantial entity, "history," if only we were not lost in foggy polemics and ideological cant.

It is not easy to find our way, as Lasch has often reminded readers, because America is so degenerate, so permeated by unreality, that few grounding principles remain visible. Lasch has long been worried about the collapse of patriarchal authority and the rise of a feminized American culture in which shallow images are valued over reality itself—a thesis that takes its most memorable shape in his popular book, *The Culture of Narcissism*.[3] The impact and celebrity of this book—the "premier work of radical social criticism in the late seventies"—have been acknowledged everywhere from *People* magazine to the White House (Clecak 46). With *The Culture of Narcissism*, Lasch proved himself the most fashionable of the contemporary nostalgic writers who have declared war on "anti-realist" modes of representation on behalf of "reality" itself. Of course, Lasch has vehemently asserted that he is *not* nostalgic; he is simply tough-minded, better yet, he is "serious." As he writes in *The Culture of Narcissism*, ". . . people today resent anyone who draws on the past in serious discussions of contemporary conditions or attempts to use the past as a standard by which to judge the present. Current critical dogma equates every such reference to the past as itself an expression of nostalgia" (Narcissism 44).

Yet if we look at Lasch's text as story, rather than as gospel, it reads as a dramatically nostalgic narration of loss. For Lasch, American culture is permeated by unreality: literary texts no longer represent the real world, faith in history has collapsed, and most important, the very selfhood of man suffers from a "narcissistic impoverishment" (Narcissism xviii). As he explains it, this narcissistic impoverishment is emblematic of the final evolution of bourgeois individualism: our contemporary hedonistic, permissive, consumer society. The self-made Protestant who once stood solidly at the center of American society has been seduced away from his own truth by a professional elite that ". . . has surrounded people with 'symbolically mediated information' and has substituted images of reality for reality itself" (Narcissism 221). This betrayal of an essential reality by what lies external to it both provokes and justifies his relentless attack on what he calls "prefabricated spectacles": modern literature, the theater of the absurd, politics, sports, education, the awareness movement. Christopher Lasch, then, would seem to align himself with a familiar radical position which claims that decadence is the ultimate expression, the end point, of bourgeois individualism and its economic and political vehicle, capitalism.

Yet Lasch insists that he parts ways not only with political conservatives but also with cultural radicals. Both groups, Lasch contends, unconsciously support the society they would criticize. In an article, "Recovering Reality," published the same year as *The Culture of Narcissism*, Lasch asserts that cultural radicals attack "bastions long since surrendered: the patriarchal family, repressive sexual morality, the conventions of literary realism" (44). The corporation, the advertising industry, and the mass culture industry have long ago co-opted these demands by replacing patriarchy with "friendly" paternalism, and the work ethic with a consumer ethic that is not only tolerant of, but deeply dependent upon constant innovation and novelty, hedonistic morality, and the rage for sexual and creative fulfillment. The conservatives, on the other hand, advocate the free expansion of the economy, thus simply encouraging more bureaucracy in both government and business. They, too, miss the right target—bureaucracy. The rise of bureaucracy has meant erosion of the standards with which Lasch is deeply sympathetic: self-sufficiency, discipline, order, sobriety, and thrifty industry.

As the values he espouses indicate, Lasch is profoundly conservative, yet he recognizes—with deep regret—that there is no returning to the "patriarchal family," to the systems of authority that he

49

sees as the only means of reinforcing those values. But though he unhappily admits his separation from a better past, Lasch will not allow himself the comfort of radical social theory and its optimistic teleology. In fact, he cannot attach himself to any political position, conservative or radical, because he sees political activity as trapped in the status quo of the present and unable to bring about real change. So, instead of trying to be explicitly political, he limits his intention to a "description" of what he calls in his subtitle "American Life in An Age of Diminishing Expectations." "Much could be written about the signs of new life in the United States. This book, however, describes a way of life that is dying . . ." (Narcissism xv).

Ranging over every aspect of American society—our literature, forms of entertainment, education, businesses, and political movements—Lasch narrates a history for each of these sectors of life which becomes a narration of degeneration and, especially, of *loss*. But the "evidence" that supports this dark cultural history is itself one of those golden myths the nostalgic writer is so fond of. Lasch believes in an ideal past: a world marked by the sobriety, enterprise, and surprisingly "appropriate" acquisitiveness of the early capitalist. Yet such a valorization of an earlier form of capitalism seems unwarranted, and is hardly persuasive; even Lasch is uneasy with it: "It is a tribute to the peculiar horror of contemporary life that it makes the worst features of earlier times—the stupefaction of the masses, the obsessed and driven lives of the bourgeoisie—seem attractive by comparison . . . . The prison life of the past looks in our own time like liberation itself" (Narcissism 99). Lasch attempts to make his idealization of "prison life" more palatable and more legitimate by claiming in his preface that "many radical movements in the past have drawn strength and sustenance from the myth or memory of a golden age in the still more distant past" (Narcissism xvii).

Myth or memory? Lasch's equivocation is revealing. Myth and memory are rhetorically opposed as alternative realms even as they collapse into the emergence of a nourishing illusion. The effect of his rhetorical gesture to keep these realms separate is that his own later narratives of the past—the sustaining illusion, if we keep in mind his preface—can then be offered as an objective account. It is no wonder, then, that Lasch speaks of nineteenth-century forms of art in glowing terms, for the central device of realism—offering an illusion as an objective truth—is his own device. Lasch conveniently neglects, or is ignorant of, the way in which writers of nineteenth-century drama and novels encouraged their audience—"Dear readers"—to consider fiction's "realism" as a rhetorical construct.

Yet nineteenth-century literature did allow the pretense of faithful mimesis to be kept up and this illusion, according to Lasch, is good because it is sustaining and nourishing. Twentieth-century art, on the other hand, is characterized as bordering upon the pathological because it puts into question the art work's previous status as a faithful copy of reality and focuses almost entirely upon its own conventions, forms, and techniques. Modern art is degenerate; the only healthy form of illusion is traditional mimesis.

This valuable mimesis is disrupted by the narcissist who is overly self-conscious and unable to suspend disbelief. And so it is not surprising that in the rise of the narcissist Lasch finds the most telling symptoms of the fatal malaise of contemporary society. Filled with nostalgia, yet incapable of learning from the past, the narcissist seeks only immediate gratification. Restless, empty, bored, the narcissist is hungry for self-knowledge yet capable of only inauthentic introspection. Deeply dependent, yet incapable of sustaining personal relationships, the narcissist has no access to a meaningful future. On the basis of a reported increase in the number of narcissistic patients in this country, Lasch generalizes his analysis of the narcissistic individual to collective behavior: "After the political turmoil of the sixties, Americans have retreated to purely personal preoccupations" (Narcissism 4). From the self-made man of earlier times, the American has decayed to the self-depleted narcissist of the present.

Lasch's view of narcissism relies on Freud's discussion of the term in his essay "On Narcissism: An Introduction." In this work, Freud opposes the narcissist, who chooses him or herself as a love object, to the individual capable of loving objects that are different from himself. (The choice of the masculine pronoun here reflects the distinction Freud makes between male development, seen as normal, and female development, seen as deviant.) According to Freud, men and women make different kinds of object-choice: real (or "anaclitic") object choice—the choice of someone different from oneself—is characteristic of men; the narcissistic type—love for someone the same as oneself—is common in women. As Stephanie Engel explains in her fine article "Femininity as Tragedy":

What is crucial for Freud in female development is, first, that the situation of the mother/infant bond sets up the preference for narcissism in future object relations and, second, that the gradual and incomplete dissolution of the pre-oedipal relationship obviates the necessity for the acquisition of a tyrannical super-ego. The violence inherent in the father's threat of castration directed toward his son creates an exacting and powerful super-ego; the little girl, by escaping that threat, is more dependent on a personally constructed agency of morality, the ego-ideal which is the legacy of her primary narcissism (85).

Engel goes on to explain how a girl's primary love for her mother, because it involves a narcissistic identification, means that she is seen as unable to develop mature relations. "This interpretation devalues psychological attributes traditionally associated with female psychology, and links 'feminine' and pathological tendencies. Thus traits such as dependency, immaturity, rigidity, and masochism have been conflated under the analytic umbrella of 'narcissism,' the psychological trademark of femininity" (Engel 88). Lasch's argument does not question Freud's assumptions about female development (nor do the contemporary analysts whose work he draws upon). Instead, he worries that men have become as narcissistic, as pathological, as women. For Lasch—as for the writers we have already discussed—the impoverishment of culture is described in sexual terms.

Freud, it must be said, is less baldly insistent on the superiority of men to women than is Lasch. At one point in his discussion, Freud describes the narcissist as possessing a self not "impoverished" but rather much too "intact." The narcissist becomes an object of apparently selfless male desire precisely because of her dependency on an ego-ideal:

It seems very evident that one person's narcissism has a great attraction for others who have renounced part of their own narcissism and are seeking after object-love . . . It is as if we envied them [women, children, animals] their power of retaining a blissful state of mind—an unassailable libido-position which we ourselves have since abandoned (Freud 70).

Though the condescending tone of this passage is irritating, it contains an important admission of the attraction of the narcissist. It is precisely such an "attraction" as Freud describes here that holds

Lasch in its power. In his longing for an "intact" self, Lasch reveals that he is captivated by the very narcissism he seems to oppose.

René Girard has explored the "incongruity" of a selfless desire for an "intact" self, an incongruity Freud acknowledges only in passing. In "Narcissism: The Freudian Myth Demythified by Proust," Girard shows that the supposedly selfless desire is for the narcissist actually a desire for a "mythic self-sufficiency."

> Nothing is more logical, therefore, than the superficially para-
> doxical conjunction of self-centeredness and other-centered-
> ness. Freud does not perceive that logic, or he refuses it because
> he insists on viewing what he calls 'object desire' as a selfless
> gesture, a deliberate and virtuous sacrifice of 'self-sufficiency,'
> rather than a fascination for an alien 'self-sufficiency,' forced
> upon us by a state of severe and involuntary deprivation in
> which human beings might generally find themselves in regard
> to that commodity (298).

The proof that human beings are "deprived" of "self-sufficiency" is the fact of their desire: "Wherever there is self-sufficiency there is no desire; the notion of a narcissistic or self-sufficient desire is a contra-diction in terms" (Girard 301).

For both Freud and Girard, the notion of desire is crucial to un-derstanding the concept of narcissism. Freud describes anaclitic object choice using the language of desire: "attraction," "seeking after," "envy." Girard insists that desire is a sign of the human ego's sense of insufficiency. And yet Lasch does not explicitly discuss "desire." When Lasch uses the *language* of desire—words such as "restless," "hungry," "empty," "searching," all of which suggest the lack that generates desire—he uses it only in describing the narcissist. (It would seem that only the narcissist has desires; Lasch does not.) There is no reason to desire: the past is irretrievable, the future is empty, the present is occupied by narcissists. And the narcissists are notably deaf: "it does no good to confront [the narcissist] with a moral argument against this incapacity or to persuade or exhort him to change his ways" (Narcissism 98). Suspicious both of his own impulse to deliver sermons and of the capacity to change on the part of those who would most benefit from his address, Lasch is apparently con-demned to an ineffectual discourse. Yet the contradiction between his claims and his aggressive rhetoric suggests that Lasch does not lack desire; he simply denies it. Maintaining the illusion of his superiority, he exalts only the self without desire. Approvingly he quotes Ivan Illich, who notes that in our time, "the ability to shape wants from experienced satisfaction becomes a rare competence . . ." (Narcissism xviii).

As Girard point out, desires do not originate in blissfully intact, "satisfied" selves. Insofar as Lasch sees narcissists everywhere—those hungry, searching, depleted selves—he inadvertently admits the inescapable connection between desire and the "insufficiency" of the self. Yet by insisting that narcissism is only a contemporary malaise, he protects himself from acknowledging his own desire, a desire that compels him to create a mythic past. How can we explain his investment in that golden past? An explanation would seem to require a revised notion of the self—one that would explain how desire, a lack within the subject, propels the subject toward the dream of an intact self. If we believe in the reality of this self, as Lasch does, we are condemned to feel guilty about our insufficiency and our desires. That is exactly what Lasch wants his readers to feel. But if we are more concerned with understanding our condition than condemning it, we need to consider notions of the self that have been articulated outside of the mainstream of American psychoanalysis, outside, that is, a humanist ideology with its belief in a true self that must be discovered and protected.

One important revised notion of the self is articulated in the writings of Jacques Lacan. In his well-known essay on the mirror stage, Lacan provides a radical psychoanalytic conception of the formation of the "I" that argues against Lasch's belief in the irreducible reality of the self. According to Lacan, the self is constituted when a child assumes the image of itself provided by a mirror. This narration of the self's formation links rather than separates self and image. "The mirror stage," says Lacan,

is a drama whose internal thrust is precipitated from insufficiency to anticipation—and which manufactures for the subject caught up in the lure of spatial identification, the succession of phantasies that extends from a fragmented body-image to a form of its totality that I shall call orthopaedic—and, lastly, to the assumption of the armour of an alienating identity, which will mark with its rigid structure the subject's entire mental development (4).

The language of this passage, with its reference to "armour" and "rigid" structure, makes the child's achievement of identity appear as a harsh process of containment, but Lacan takes pains to insist that the fixing of identity in first one and then other images is what makes subjectivity possible. Further, this history of the self makes "jubilant" the moment when the child attaches itself to a specular image without recognizing that the "I" is objectified in something alien to itself. Lacan, then, not only provides the self with a moment in which it obtains a satisfying unity with the image that constitutes it, but also insists that we depend on images—on the symbolic order Lasch so detests—to shape our identity.[4] Indeed, Lacan argues that Freud's work, with its emphasis on the importance of language and the unconscious, also elaborates the *construction* rather than the true reality of the self.

Lasch's history of the constitution of the psyche depends on a dichotomy between a self based in reality, the proper self of the past, and one that is wholly fictional, the narcissistic self. The proper self of the past, he says, was able to internalize images of authority that guaranteed a sense of reality by inhibiting the archaic and aggressive fantasies of the id. The superego, thus formed and strengthened, became a guarantor of reality. When these authoritative images are not incorporated, as he says they are not at the present, the superego apparently becomes as fantastic as the id. Notice that the earlier self follows a male pattern of development, the narcissist the path of the female. The opposition between past and present selves is explicitly a sexual opposition that valorizes male over female, and thus past over present. In his chapter "Changing Modes of Making It: From Horatio Alger to the Happy Hooker," Lasch's description of the past describes only how "young men" were expected to achieve success. He does not even use the female pronoun until he begins to discuss the cultural decline of the seventies. The opposition between male and female, past and present serves Lasch well, enabling him to disguise the images that constitute the proper self in the first place. Similarly, by opposing the "past" to the "present," he hopes to privilege the former while avoiding questions about just how this "past" has been constructed.

Lasch's aggressively antithetical system of representation relies not only upon keeping a whole series of realms opposed and separated (life and art, reality and image, work and play, self and other, male and female) but also on keeping the term on the left as a referent of the term on the right. And so the narcissist becomes the whore, for narcissists—be they experimental novelists, advertising executives, corporation presidents, cultural radicals, black pride advocates, or feminists—are notably unfaithful to the referent and responsible for its loss.

The self-controlled male of the nineteenth century, in other words, has given way to the self-indulgent woman of the present. In our time, Lasch reports, "the happy hooker stands in place of Horatio Alger as the prototype of personal success. If Robinson Crusoe embodied the ideal type of economic man, the hero of bourgeois society in its ascendancy, the spirit of Moll Flanders presides over its dotage" (Narcissism 53). Surely this opposition of Robinson Crusoe to Moll Flanders is odd, since both characters are exemplary figures of 18th-century capitalism.[5] But Lasch is not concerned with history here. He simply wants readers to make a negative judgment of women as immoral and self-serving—as shameless prostitutes—so that readers will have the proper attitude toward the present.

The prostitute, then, is Lasch's prototype of the narcissistic American. She serves as a figure of sin and decadence that allows Lasch—and presumably the reader—to show that he is, by contrast, good, male, and not easily seduced.

> In the seventies . . . it appears that the prostitute . . . best exemplifies the qualities indispensable to success in American society. She . . . sells herself for a living. . . . She craves admiration but scorns those who provide it and thus derives little gratification from her social successes. The fact that she lives in a milieu of interpersonal relations does not make her a conformist or "other-directed" type. She remains a loner, dependent on others only as a hawk depends on chickens. She exploits the ethic of pleasure that has replaced the ethic of achievement, but her career more than any other reminds us that contemporary hedonism, of which she is the supreme symbol, orginates . . . in a war of all against all . . . (Narcissism 64–65).

Significantly, what gets lost in this diatribe is the fact that men exploit prostitutes; according to Lasch, it is the prostitute who does the exploiting. And her attempt to find some measure of independence and positive meaning—the hooker is "happy"—is seen by Lasch as a sign of her depravity and cruelly predatory nature. By this, we are meant to understand that the attachment of feminine sexuality to pleasure

B y the time the *The Culture of Narcissism* had been published in 1978, John Irving's *The World According to Garp* was already becoming a phenomenon, a cult novel. What would Lasch think of it? Not only does the novel depict "feminized" men, but it also values "imagination" over "reality" and is quite self-conscious about its strategies. All of this suggests that *The World According to Garp* might be one of those books that subverts the hegemony of male authority and the nostalgic desire for fixed sexual difference. But it is not. Despite the novel's thematic concerns, *Garp*'s narrative strategies are conservative: they construct a defense against feminism. Irving, like the other writers we have discussed, is involved in a struggle over *who can speak*. His novel pits male authority against female authority, asserting the triumph of the male writer even in his death.

Garp, the hero of Irving's best-seller, receives this rave review for one of his own books: "The women's movement has at last exhibited a significant influence on a significant male writer" (476). Irving's *Garp* begs for a similar review. It sympathetically discusses feminist issues—rape, single motherhood, the aspirations of women for political power, domestic role reversal. In a gesture toward androgyny, it provides characters who prove the viability of transsexuality. Its major women characters are strong and capable. Garp's mother, Jenny Fields, is a champion of feminists; she authors her life and insists upon directing her own destiny. Garp's wife Helen, is an exemplar of intelligence and cool professionalism. She supports the family while Garp minds the children, cooks, and cleans—an arrangement that satisfies them both. In other words, *Garp* seems to meet early feminist prescriptions that the novel "achieve cultural androgyny," provide "role models," and "[augment] consciousness raising" (Register 13).

Yet even a cursory feminist analysis reveals the novel's strong ambivalence about feminism. All of the strong female characters in the novel are uncomfortable with the label "feminist," although, in their words, they are "not antifeminist!" (552). The narrator explains that Jenny "felt discomfort at the word *feminism*. She was not sure what it meant but the *word* reminded her of feminine hygiene and the Valentine treatment"—the torturous treatment for syphilis in males (185). In the novel, "feminism" always designates a simplistic ideology, and those who embrace it are extremists. In a 1982 review of the "Garp" phenomenon, Marilyn French noted that the villains of the book are feminists, pictured as full of a hate for men that precipitates acts of violence. As French says, in the novel "sex, violence, and feminism" are conflated (14). French claims that Irving's "vision" is unreal—"its world is not mine"—and explains that its falsification of feminism is the result of a drastically limited canvas that features a small domestic sphere and excludes the larger public context (16). But a strong antagonism to feminism is built into the novel's form, not just into a personal "vision" that can be opposed to the "truth" about feminists. Understanding this may help us see why Garp is so insistent about defending narrative *structure*.

At first it seems that *The World According to Garp* defends *women's* right to authority. It begins with the figure of a strong matriarch, Garp's mother, Jenny. She competently defends herself against "male lust" and staunchly commits herself to single motherhood, thus undercutting the male's traditional rights over her body and his place as head of the family. She is neither a dutiful daughter nor anyone's wife, and we are encouraged to admire her because of this. Further-more, she recounts her rebellion against traditional sex roles in an autobiography that "was said to bridge the usual gap between literary merit and popularity" (13). The book, entitled *A Sexual Suspect*, is popular because it speaks for a multitude of women who soon become Jenny's followers. All this seems to suggest that women can have control over themselves and writing. But what is the status of Jenny's writing?

Although she is an influential writer, Jenny's book is "no literary jewel" (168). Garp puts it more bluntly when he says that the book has "the same literary merit as the Sears Roebuck catalog" (13). His metaphor points out what he considers to be the book's main flaws: a mundane prose style and simple-minded organizational scheme. The only way that Jenny can bind her story together ("the way fog shrouds an uneven landscape," the narrator tells us [157]) is with this opening sentence: "In this dirty-minded world, you are either somebody's wife or somebody's whore, or fast on the way of becom-ing one or the other" (157). This sentence provides the book with a unity of tone—strident assertiveness—presumably appropriate to her thesis: the right of individual women to refuse their two traditional options. Garp's literary assessment of Jenny's style thus becomes an unspoken commentary on her thesis. We are led to believe that Jen-ny's literal prose style is evidence of a dogmatic and somewhat sim-ple-minded view of the world. "Disharmonious," "rambling," "messy" (157–58), Jenny's book is a testament to her failure to pro-duce a truly coherent work that could capture what is privileged in the novel, the "complexity of human behavior." Unlike "art," *A Sex-ual Suspect* can only catalog experience—it is, as Jenny describes it, "about me" (183)—and render this personal experience in a literal-minded way.[1]

Jenny is the central woman character in the novel, and *A Sexual Suspect* is the book's most powerful instance of women's writing. In order to limit the authority of this writing, however, the novel retains (precisely in order to denounce it) the idea of "literal writing." The notion that literal writing even exists rests upon the assumption that language is transparent so that words are able to represent accurately their referents, the world or the self. This assumption informs much literary criticism, including feminist literary criticism that valorizes those kinds of women's writing that are somehow particularly close to life. Elizabeth Janeway, for example, writes in *The Harvard Guide to Contemporary American Writing* that "If there is a woman's literature, it will derive from an area of experience, worthy of exploration which is known pretty exclusively to women and largely overlooked by men" (342). She goes on to say that "an authentic literature reflects actual life" (346). Janeway's second statement, less cautious than her first, binds her to a view of literature that Irving easily denounces in the name of "art," although, as we will show, his "art" also claims to represent the world. It is in his interest to set up a false opposition between art and experience in order to give his own writing a special value. Literature based solely on experience is proved, through Jenny's book, to be shapeless and timebound. Her messy story is timely but ephemeral: after Jenny's death, *A Sexual Suspect* is never printed again. Irving further critiques "literature that reflects actual life" by suggesting that the writer devoted to actual life cannot sustain the act of writing: having captured and depleted her subject matter—"me"—Jenny has no more to write.

In *The World According to Garp*, autobiographical writing is called the "worst" kind of writing (457). With this judgment, the most powerful form of women's writing in the novel is discredited. But to be fair, *Garp* does provide alternative forms of writing by "better" women writers, though these alternatives are withdrawn as soon as they are offered. One character, Alice, writes beautifully. She cares about language as a thing in itself, rather than as a mere tool for reflecting life, but she is unable to finish a single novel. Another, Ellen James, is a good poet. But her collection of poems, *Speeches Delivered to Animals and Flowers*, and her genre, the lyric poem, are made to seem peripheral in a novel whose very subject matter privileges the narrative rendering of complex human behavior.

The writing of the major male character, Garp, is set in opposition to the writing of all these women. It is imaginative rather than literal, beautifully styled, complete and complex—in short, it makes Garp into what the narrator calls a "real writer" (223). The opposition between male and female writing is set in sharpest relief at the beginning of the novel through the contrast of Jenny's writing with Garp's. Irving juxtaposes the ease with which Jenny steadily produces her 1,158-page life story with the difficulty with which T. S. Garp writes a short story that has very little to do with his own experience. While Jenny's story comes from memory, Garp's story, "The Pension Grillparzer," is drawn from an interior source that is privileged in the novel—imagination. "Imagination," Garp realized, "came harder than memory" (124). Though serious reviewers "chide" Jenny for "her actual writing" (185), her book becomes a "household product"

(195). Garp's story, on the other hand, "would first appear in a serious journal where nobody would read it" (169). Even though he initially lacks an audience, Garp's is the more fecund mode of writing. "The Pension Grillparzer" is the first of several serious stories published in a serious way that culminate in a book, *The World According to Bensenhaver*, which wins him everything: it is both serious and popular. Still, because it is so "imaginative," "The Pension Grillparzer" is considered his best work by everyone in the novel whose judgment seriously counts. This high evaluation of Garp's work, juxtaposed with derogatory remarks about Jenny's book, is Irving's way of teaching us the importance of "imagination" in writing. It is a lesson repeated over and over in the novel.

All that is said about imaginative fiction in *Garp* invites the reader to admire rather than understand it. As in literal writing, language in the fictional work is transparent; but fiction's referent is different: literal writing reveals the "real world" whereas good fiction reveals "imagination." Claiming that a work is "imaginative" is an important maneuver since distancing writing from the world elevates the work's status. The "imaginative" work is freed from the exigencies of history and thus enters the realm of eternal objects. Furthermore, the apparent autonomy of the imaginative work insures its "wholeness"; imaginative work is true to itself. This "inner truth" must be worshipped rather than articulated. Reviewers who use reductive strategies of interpretation are the objects of Garp's scorn: he mutters about "The destruction of art by sociology and psychoanalysis" (525). Immutable, whole, true, the work of art is "better" than the known and knowable world.

Yet for all of Garp's insistence on the separateness of the imaginative work, he also claims that it is "better" than literal-minded fiction because it is *closer* to the world. How are we to explain this seeming paradox? Apparently the creation of an autonomous work requires such mastery and artistry that the result is assured of being mysteriously complex. And since life itself is mysterious and complex, the work is true to life. This logic bestows a god-like power on the author and helps us to accept the *thesis* that art is a sacred ideal. For all his efforts to differentiate fictional and literal writing, the two forms converge: Garp insistently promotes a theory of writing that depends on his notion of "reality"—his writing, we are encouraged to believe, is the "real" thing. Lasch thinks literature should reproduce history; Irving embraces literature that is imaginative. But both want the same thing: a serious realm of writing, produced by men, that brings us "reality."

What is women's relationship to this valorized realm of writing? In the novel, women are destined to consume rather than produce "art." Garp, the incarnation of the active male imagination, is a "natural storyteller" (155), while his audience consists of women who, like his wife Helen, seem to be "natural" spectators for this writing. Jenny, a prolific "bad" writer, is simply awed by "real writing." Upon reading her son's first story, "Jenny marvelled at her son's imagination" (170). She is not only awed, but silenced: she reads many books, but "she had nothing to say about them" (36). Helen, too, is a voracious reader, one who acknowledges she cannot write. Nevertheless, her fine critical intelligence allows her to appreciate fully works of the imagination. In fact, all of the women readers—including Alice, the babysitter Cindy, and Mrs. Ralph—are cast into the role of born consumers and spectators, awed and seduced by the display of male authority.

Men, on the other hand, are active, productive readers and writers. Garp reads only to produce fiction and writes fiction to seduce women. When Garp's writing does not seduce women—be it Helen, Alice, or Cindy—it still functions procreatively, as a means of increasing his family. At the end of the novel, Garp attracts Ellen James by means of *The World According to Bensenhaver* and eventually adopts her. *The World According to Garp* clearly advocates, then, a familiar dichotomy between an active male principle and a passive female principle. This familiar sexual dichotomy, assumed by the novel to be a fact of nature, determines who will write and who will read. "Real" writing, in this novel, is intimately connected with the "active" male and his sexuality.

It is not only this particular novel, of course, that claims only men can produce "art." Men have long appropriated the power of writing by maintaining as natural and inevitable the metaphorical link between pen and penis, author and patriarch.[2] Moreover, modern theorists of the novel argue that narrative structure reinforces both these metaphorical connections and paternal themes. Describing a symbiotic relationship between form and content, Edward Said argues that the novel is often *about* a generational conflict between father and son, a conflict that initiates the son's search for identity. But the figure of the father also guarantees form, namely narrative sequence, coherence, integrity. "The novel," Said writes, "most explicitly realizes these conventions, gives them coherence and imaginative life by grounding them in a text whose beginning premise is paternal" (163). If the beginning premise of the novel's logic is paternal, so too, Peter Brooks would argue, is its conclusion. He writes that "All narrative must, as a system of meaning, conceive itself as essentially retrospective. Only the sons can tell the story of the fathers. Narrative, like geneaology, is a matter of patronymics" (301). Conceptualized in terms of paternal geneaology, narrative sequence insures the discovery of identity in its linear, consecutive explanation of events. Events unfold over time and gather significance in a conclusion that provides retrospective coherence. We can infer from this argument that traditional narrative form, though not essentially "male," is not neutral: it preserves a patriarchal concept of identity as coherent and univocal, a concept that has most often privileged male identity and authority. Of course, one cannot fully subscribe to Brooks's adamantly restricted view of the novel ("only *sons* can tell the story of the fathers") without considering his limited evidence; both he and Said omit all analysis of women novelists. The truth of Said's and Brooks's proclamations, however, concerns us less, here, than the point that these arguments coincide with, and can illuminate, Irving's defense of traditional narrative structure.[3]

Both Said's and Brooks's analyses suggest that the story of Oedipus is the paradigm for narrative structure. Roland Barthes confirms this when he tells us that without Oedipus story-telling is impossible:

> If there is no longer a Father, why tell stories? Doesn't every narrative lead back to Oedipus? Isn't storytelling always a way of searching for one's origins, speaking one's conflicts with the Law, entering into the dialectic of tenderness and hatred? . . . As fiction, Oedipus was at least good for something: to make good novels, to tell good stories (*The Pleasure of the Text* 47).

The passage from ignorance to knowledge, the familiar trajectory of the realistic novel, reenacts the oedipal drama. The plot of *The World According to Garp*, too, reproduces this rite of passage. It is the story of the life and development of a male writer, who, by learning his craft, which entails writing stories that become more and more obviously the oedipal story (*My Father's Illusions* is his last novel), finally acquires patriarchal authority.

Analyses of narrative structure like Said's and Brooks's insist that narrative logic reproduces the oedipal trajectory. But these analyses

71

always ignore the fact that the oedipal trajectory is specifically dependent upon the discovery of sexual difference. In the oedipal drama, the son moves from the naive assumption that everyone has a penis to the discovery of women's lack of one. This discovery of castration and the anxiety it provokes propel him towards reconciliation with the Law of the Father, the Symbolic Order. *Garp* literally represents what the structure of this drama depends upon: the fear of castration and the corresponding insistence upon sexual difference defined by "castration" (or lack). This fear is represented when Helen bites off Michael Milton's penis; but more threatening to Garp is the graphic equation of castration and silence in the figures of the Ellen Jamesians—women who cut off their own tongues. Here women seem to choose what the oedipal drama makes necessary: women are defined by silence and by a lack that is perceived as mutilation. The familiar trajectory of the novel, then, depends as much upon the drama of silencing and castrating (mutilating) the female as it does upon reconciling the son to the father. If Oedipus is the paradigm for narrative structure, then it is the demands of narrative structure itself that inscribe, not only men's authority and women's silence, but the violence done to women as well.

Irving not only relies on this structure but defends it in a way that Barthes does not. Barthes poses his questions about the death of the father and its consequences for narrative as part of a meditation on modern writing that both performs and subverts the conventions of traditional narrative. In some sense, *The World According to Garp* is also a meditation on the death of the father and its consequences for narrative and the male writer. Certainly because it is about the development of a writer, the book has occasion to perform and comment upon the conventions of narrative writing. *Garp* opens with the death of the father (Garp's), as do many nineteenth-century novels that begin by presenting the reader with fatherless orphans. But unlike the nineteenth-century novel, *Garp* connects the death of the father to the rise of women, particularly the rise of the mother to power. In response to this shift of power, Garp, like the nostalgic writers we have already discussed, becomes more and more adamant about protecting patriarchy, not only by equating "real writing" with male writing, but also by protecting traditional narrative conventions. Again the battleground is representation; Irving lets his hero do battle for him.

One of Garp's early experiences demonstrates Irving's defensive response to challenges to traditional conventions. When the young

ents—reality, honesty, truth—that she links with the Puritan past, hardworking women, and canonical texts written by men. So intent is she on opposing false writing to true writing that she neglects to ask whose interests are served by her advocacy of certain conventions of writing.

Douglas's nostalgic text reaches a conclusion that is finally as abject as Lasch's: the feminization of American life makes male power stronger by debilitating serious thought and writing. Lasch, almost literally taking a page from Douglas's book, also insists that the feminization of culture produces an even more oppressive society ruled by the father, the "New Paternalism." But contemporary efforts to undo the oppositions and hierarchies so valued by both Douglas and Lasch can be read much differently than they do. The oppositions of high art to low art, male to female, reality to image all help maintain the authority of the patriarchal status quo by disguising the structures that protect its cherished truths. Revealing the operation of oppressive systems of representation, experimenting with new forms, at least allows for the possibility of subversion. Lasch is more accurate than he knows when he writes in his preface: "Much more could be written about signs of new life in the United States. This book, however, describes a way of life that is dying . . ." (xv). Or better, a privileged "reality" that is dying. The signs of new life cannot be spoken by Lasch because they subvert the antitheses—real and non-real, past and present, male and female—on which his text depends. It is in the play of figures—figures not so rigidly opposed to each other—that a new symbolic order will be articulated. Lasch almost knows this. In one of the few quiet moments in his text he remarks: "It does not seem unreasonable to believe, even in the political passivity and quietism of the 1970s, that a thoroughgoing transformation of our social arrangements remains a possibility . . ." (Narcissism 206). This assertion receives no elaboration.

The New York Times Bestseller List described *The Culture of Narcissism* as a "hellfire sermon on the decay permeating American life." It was lodged for weeks between two self-help books: a volume that proposed yet another way to prevent decay (by extolling the joy of running), and a book that Lasch would undoubtedly deem worthy of a puritanical sermon—*How to Get Everything You Want Out of Life*. The placement of his text is easy to explain. Lasch's refusal of what he calls the "modernist esthetic," a refusal of the possibilities created by new modes of discourse, condemns him to repeat the discourse

value" and the home was "an important part of the commercial production process" (5). Her thesis is that the economic pressures of capitalism turned busy, independent women into narcissistic, sentimental consumers. Women have become "the subconscious of capitalist culture" that guarantees the continuance of male hegemony (Douglas 67).

In a section of the book entitled "The End of Mother Power" (shades of the myth of the Amazon), Douglas finds examples of the old and the new woman in the contrast between the mother and wife of one Horace Bushnell. Bushnell's mother is a strong and hardworking woman whose labor in the home is "economically indispensable" (53). His wife does not work. She is a charming, educated, ministering angel—one of those women who would soon join a legion of "liberal ministers and literary women" that would shape Americans into consumers (77). While Douglas claims not to idealize Bushnell's hardworking mother, her whole book is dedicated to the proposition that an alliance of women, ministers, and the printing press led to the disavowal of "masculine" reality and feminine toughness. And the major vehicle of this "disestablishment" of the real is feminine writing: "Where will the process of feminization, of fictionalization stop?" (Douglas 117).

Once again the proliferation of women's writing is made the cause of cultural decline, but this time in the text of a feminist scholar. Because Douglas, unlike Lasch, is aware of the oppressiveness of the very polarity between masculine and feminine upon which she relies, she takes pains not to naturalize it. She places quotations around "masculine" and "feminine" whenever she uses the words. She explains that women were not to blame for their insidious role—they were victims of the culture even as they produced it. Yet Douglas also insists that tough-minded feminists like herself must stand at a distance from these deluded, "damaged" women: explain them and recognize "the price" of what has been lost—sexuality, equality, and an "honest culture" (329). Of course, to stand where she does requires strategies of nostalgia, a sentiment she abhors, and an implicit "siding with the enemy" (Douglas 11). As Jane Tompkins puts it: "In sum, despite her apparent rejection of capitalism and the *status quo*, the attitude Douglas expresses toward the vast quantity of literature written by women . . . is contempt. The query one hears behind every page of her indictment of feminization is: why can't a woman be more like a man?" (181). We put it a bit differently. Douglas blames women, particularly women writers, for challenging longed for, stable refer-

mother as a ravenous monster, make it impossible for the child to synthesize "good" and "bad" parental images. In his fear of aggression from the bad parents—projections of his own rage— he idealizes the good parents who will come to the rescue (Narcissism 38).

The father's intervention is needed to bring at least the male child out of this pre-oedipal phase. The terrible women that Lasch believes now populate the imagination are proof, then, of Lasch's thesis that the father's loss of authority has a terrible effect—the mother gains rage-provoking power. Lasch claims that the proliferation of monstrous images of the mother, an expression of rage against "the female sex," only "superficially represents a defensive male reaction against feminism" (Narcissism 205); but we have seen in the previous chapter that challenges to male authority and prerogatives made in and by "various organs . . . of Women's Liberation" have clearly provoked some male writers to imagine women as monsters who must be conquered (Stade 24).

It is not only the movement of women into the castrating role of the father that Lasch finds horrible. Worse still is what he sees as the corresponding shift of men into the position of women. Lasch interprets the shifting location of men and women within the model of male domination because he cannot imagine relations that are not hierarchical and antithetical. And so men now must suffer the condition of dominated women. The "New Paternalism," the managerial and professional elite, gives us all the degraded status of women— oppressed, dependent, self-less and therefore in constant need of others to reassure us of our existence. Today, as Lasch puts it, "men and women *alike* [our emphasis] have to project an attractive image and to become simultaneously role players and connoisseurs of their own performance" (Narcissism 92).

Lasch's book linked the feminization and the degradation of culture one year after the publication of Ann Douglas's *The Feminization of American Culture*. Both books are part of the same discursive network. Like the *Culture of Narcissism, The Feminization of American Culture* mourns the loss of a past moment when intellectual life possessed a "toughness, a sternness, an intellectual rigor" (Douglas 18). But Douglas is a self-proclaimed feminist who asserts that, in the past, gender arrangements were more nearly equal. Before capitalism, says Douglas, "the independent woman" was considered of "highest

and power is a mark of the decay of society. In the past at least, women were repressed and civilized: the American pioneer, says Lasch, "imagined that his offspring, raised under the morally refining influence of feminine 'culture,' would grow up to be sober, law-abiding, domesticated American citizens" (Narcissism 11). Now, it seems, men have replaced women as morally superior beings.

The myth of the self-controlled male and the self-absorbed female—the happy hooker—is authorized by Freud's essay on narcissism, a work in which Freud creates the figures of the selfless man and the marvelous but self-centered woman he desires. In Freud's view, this sexual incongruity produces a domestic tragedy: man loves a woman who cannot love him in return. But a man can assuage his disappointment in love with the knowledge that he has renounced narcissism and is therefore morally superior to the woman who scorns him. In Freud's scenario, then, woman occupies both the desired place of the intact self and the condemned position of the shallow narcissist. As Lasch points out, contemporary feminists have called into question this combined image of degradation and idealization; but their question is actually a profound threat. What happens when woman is no longer content with her place? When woman moves out of her "proper" position—a position never as "proper" as the male position that stands opposed to her deviant one—she breaks the mirror of mimesis that establishes the "reality" of male identity, and shatters the illusion of his superiority. When this happens, we move into the reign of woman.

And for Lasch, the reign of woman is equally destructive of men and women. Women are deprived of the limited but secure social role that formerly protected them from male violence; men are increasingly impotent, having acquired a terrible fear of women: "the cruel, destructive, domineering woman, la belle dame sans merci, has moved from the periphery of literature and other arts to a position close to the center" (Narcissism 203). The "cruel, destructive, domineering woman" has all the traits of the castrating mother. Lasch earlier makes clear that the weakening of the oedipal triangle has made the mother increasingly dominant and threatening to male identity. She is, in fact, at the origin of pathological narcissism. Using the work of Melanie Klein to explain the mother's role, Lasch writes:

early feelings of overpowering rage, directed especially against the mother and secondarily against the internalized image of the

of the experts he berates. Those experts, like Lasch, insist that they can bring "reality" to readers and help them discover their true selves.

But perhaps Lasch's sense of an ending marks the close of the seemingly faithful language of mimesis he produces and decries. This mode of representation gained its authority by asserting the inauthenticity of the speech of others while denying its own artifice. By exposing this strategy, "antirealists" haave indeed subverted the power of traditional mimesis but they have not, as Lasch insists, repudiated politics. Without challenging the authoritarian ideologies that disguise themselves as "reality," as nature itself, how can a writer hope to be political? Paradoxically, it is Lasch the "realist" who retreats from politics in the name of a mythically golden past. And so he is melancholy and nostalgic. But the reader of *The Culture of Narcissism* may feel otherwise. Recorded in this book is the rise of a language located beyond the rhetoric of the "real"—a language that hopes to articulate new relations between men and women, self and other.

Chapter
Three

Women
and the
Word
According
to
Garp

Garp submits his first story for publication, it is rejected by one journal because the story "does nothing new with language or with form" (181). Puzzled, Garp consults his teacher, Mr. Tinch, who taught him how to write by teaching him respect for "good old grammar" (93). But Mr. Tinch, who reeks of death and decay, is simply as puzzled as Garp. The rotting Mr. Tinch seems to embody Irving's awareness of the decay of old-fashioned standards and conventions. Nevertheless, Irving valorizes Garp's adherence to traditional narrative with its insistence on sexual difference and the privileged status of male writing. When Garp's writing becomes more "successful" (i.e., popular), the same journal requests one of his stories. Garp triumphantly shoots back a nasty rejection on the rejection slip he had received so many years ago: "I am still doing nothing new with language or with form. Thanks for asking me though" (182). Success has vindicated Garp's inflexible attitude toward form. Experimenting with narrative convention, we are meant to understand, is simply a fad. What really counts—to everybody—is success, which itself becomes a validation for the truth of traditional narrative form.

By adhering to conventions that meet expectations and insure our pleasure, a writer is likely to be successful. Unconventional writing sacrifices the pleasure of structuring meaning in familiar ways and, by doing so, challenges the status of any particular meaning as absolute. Irving cannot acknowledge that conventions of writing create the impression of truth because that acknowledgment would threaten his belief in his own truthfulness and seriousness. For Irving, narrative structure is a natural way to achieve and reflect the truth. But narrative is not natural; Irving simply naturalizes an important narrative convention—the convention of narrative sequence, of the significant accumulation of events toward an inevitable "truth." Thus Irving's conventionalism, which parallels Garp's, becomes a way of defending his own seriousness and a success that accompanies his adherence to the familiar.

Garp achieves his success with a book entitled *The World According to Bensenhaver*. Both the book's title and its major concerns, of course, are meant to mirror *The World According to Garp*. The sequence of events in both books is generated by sexual violence: both depend upon erotic polarization, and the violence that ensues from it, to make things happen. At the beginning of *The World According to Bensenhaver* Hope Standish is raped. *The World According to Garp* is powered by a first sentence that sets men and women in opposition: "Garp's mother, Jenny Fields, was arrested in Boston in 1942, for wounding a man in a movie theatre" (1). A simple plot summary demonstrates that the rest of the novel continues to rely on the war between the sexes: Jenny does not want to have anything to do with men. She writes a book in defense of this position. Her book attracts a group of feminist extremists, the Ellen Jamesians, to Jenny and Garp. These women have banded together to make the raped and mutilated Ellen James (a modern Philomela) a political cause, and in the end one of them kills Garp. The battle of the sexes is reproduced within Garp's family where sexual tensions between Garp and Helen lead to a catastrophe in which Helen sexually mutilates a man and Garp kills one of his own children. In sum, sexual violence is what happens in the novel.

In both the worlds of Garp and Bensenhaver, the sequence of events seems contrived to fulfill the popular demand for violence, but Irving works to extol the "seriousness" of his violent narrative by defending the seriousness of Garp's novel. Jillsey Sloper, in her defense of *The World According to Bensenhaver*, acts as Irving's mouthpiece. Jillsey Sloper is a reader who has an intuitive access to what makes a work popular as well as a feeling for the deeper truths of literature. She finds "sick" (i.e., violent) books compelling: ". . . this book is so *sick* you *know* somethin's gonna happen, but you can't imagine *what*" (452). But she dignifies this perversity by saying that "It feels so *true*" (453). The narrator comments later that Jillsey uses "true" in the "good way," "not as in 'real life'." (457). Here we have it again: Garp's writing is not based upon life, and yet it is a perfect representation of it; as Jillsey explains, with "true" books one can say, "Yeah! That's just how damned people *behave* all the time!" (453).

There are several "truths" being defended here. One is that Garp is a serious writer, who can capture the "truth" of human behavior. Another is that narrative sequence, what happens, is natural—there is a compelling human "instinct" to want to know what happens—and this narrative sequence is fully adequate to expressing human behavior. (Elsewhere, Garp wonders: "What is the instinct in people that makes them expect something to happen?" [265]). Finally, male power is necessary and inevitable, and so sexual violence is as well. For their "truth," Irving and Garp depend upon the "naturalness" of an active male principle and a passive female principle, a polarization similar to those we have analyzed in other texts. This particular opposition, however, is erotic, violent, hierarchical, giving rise to women's victimization. Irving's narrator is clearly unhappy about this victimization and insists on decrying male violence in the form of rape. It doesn't matter. Irving's explanation for rape, finally, is male lust, an extreme form of the active male principle. Rape, then, is another consequence of the facts of nature. And in the figure of the Ellen Jamesians, who cut off their own tongues in sympathy with Ellen James, Irving entertains the notion that the extreme of female "nature"—masochism—is also a cause of the victimization of women. This victimization in turn generates a "natural" sequence of events—a true narrative. Narrative is naturalized, is itself the truth.

Since in classical narrative it is so important to know "what happens," and to know the *meaning* of what happens, the conclusion is always privileged. "Truth, these [traditional] narratives tell us, is *at the end* of expectation" (Barthes, *S/Z* 76). This truth is conventionally embodied in the hero's death, the moment when meaning is conferred upon his entire life, giving the narrative—normally the story of his life—coherence as well. "A novelist is a doctor who sees only terminal cases" (570) is the way Garp chooses to formulate this convention. Having naturalized narrative sequence by naturalizing violence between the sexes, Irving makes the novel's conventional momentum toward death seem inevitable. Our hero, Garp, must die as a result of sexual violence, and his death confers meaning upon the novel.

If we were to pay attention only to the subject matter, it would seem as though Irving were proposing something like the following: Feminism is exacerbating the battle between the sexes, bringing more violence into society. The best-intentioned men are becoming weaker, are less emotionally capable of dealing with this violence. They are mutilated or killed—they cannot endure. The best of women are stronger. They deal with violence wisely and they will survive, just as Helen and Hope do. But when we see the importance of the form of narrative, when we understand that death is what confers meaning on the whole of narrative, we read differently: Irving is saying that the survival of women is insignificant since men will endure in more important ways. Garp's death serves only to make his life more important. In death, Garp becomes the all-powerful father he could never quite be in life.

The last chapter of *The World According to Garp*, "Life After Garp," tells how the surviving characters of the novel devote the rest of their lives to making Garp's own life more important and meaningful: by remembering it. Helen, Roberta, Duncan, Jenny, various biographers and critics, all join in a chorus singing Garp's praises. Having apparently conceded the loss of the father at the beginning of his novel,

Irving now redeems that loss. The father, when his death is framed by the traditional novel, simply becomes more important.

Analyzing traditional narrative conventions teaches us how the death of the father can make him larger than life. Paradoxically, patriarchy can be served by assaults on it (as we have seen in the heroics of those who fight the Amazon) and this means that feminism can be made the obstacle to its own ends. In *Garp*, the death of the father at the hands of a feminist extremist dignifies the hero at the expense of feminist ideology; but Irving also uses the feminist issue of rape to entrench patriarchal power by making sexual violence seem "natural" and by exploiting it to generate and naturalize narrative sequence. Irving easily writes a text that meets thematic criteria for the "feminist" novel—he includes strong female characters who are attractive survivors—without ever jeopardizing the patriarchal power inscribed in traditional narrative conventions. So rather than concentrating on whether or not a work of fiction truthfully represents women—a critical focus that assumes a transparent writing is possible—feminist critics should examine how writing creates the illusion of truth. In the novel in general, and in *The World According to Garp* in particular, truth is structured in such a way as to guarantee paternal authority and to silence women, no matter how much they may seem to speak.

Chapter
Four

The
Anxiety
of
Feminist
Influence

A pas-
sionate urgency permeates Harold Bloom's
works, an urgency motivated by a sense of
loss and cultural decline. He, like the "strong poets" he describes, is
engaged in a battle against the death of Poetry, and by "Poetry" he
means a tradition, a line of influence that shapes a poet's voice, his
very identity. According to Bloom, we must either acknowledge the
tradition of influence he reveals or participate in the destruction of
poetry itself. In *A Map of Misreading* (1975), Bloom tells us that he
does not relish the task of bearing the bad tidings, this "Gospel of
Gloom," as he calls it, but we can no longer evade the fact that "our
mutual sense of canonical standards has undergone a remarkable
dimming, a fading into the light of a common garishness" (36). What
we are in danger of losing, then, is a sense of the importance of the
past, of the power of the traditional literary canon. The traditional
canon is, of course, male, preserved and perpetuated by strong male

81

poets. Like Ann Douglas and John Irving, Bloom writes to inspire admiration for the power of the father's writing.

Most of the work of feminist literary critics has been to question this exclusion of women writers from the canon. Not surprisingly, Bloom suggests that "the literature of Women's Liberation" is implicated in "the excessively volatile senses-of-tradition that have made canon-formation so uncertain a process . . . particularly during the last twenty years" (MM 36). Bloom's response to these volatile redefinitions of the canon is to insist not only upon the traditional canon, but upon a story of its perpetuation that makes this canon seem inevitable and necessary. As the story unfolds, it becomes clear whose "volatile" redefinitions are the most threatening, for the story is insistently patriarchal, delineating a struggle between fathers and sons that depends for its power upon Freud's family romance, a story that is an explanation for the formation of male identity.

The chauvinism of Bloom's explanatory model has not been lost on feminist critics. Annette Kolodny argues that the psychodynamics of Bloom's paradigm render women invisible except as whore/mother Muses to male power, and argues for "another tradition entirely," "that in which women taught one another how to read and write about and out of their own unique (and sometimes isolated) contexts" (465).[1] Other feminist literary critics have also responded to Bloom's male paradigm of literary influence by calling for a different, female paradigm. Our analysis addresses the problematic assumption of grounding writing in these sexual oppositions both Bloom and his feminist critics advocate.

But is Bloom really capable of articulating a closed masculine system? Bloom's paradigm is a defense against the feminization of authority, but a defense that finally bends and cracks under the passionate attempt to make it work. Though Bloom's narrative is designed to create the illusion of an autonomous male sphere of self and text, Bloom fails in his efforts to repress the feminine, which for him is the other that threatens masculine identity. As Bloom himself says, repression "is anything but a liberating process" (*The Anxiety of Influence* 107). His text becomes increasingly immersed in the feminine and the feminization of authority, in spite of his energetic effort to defend himself against such a force.

At first it seems that Bloom has nothing to say about femininity. In *The Anxiety of Influence*, Bloom delineates a young poet's struggle to attain his own poetic identity and to "rescue" a Muse from his precursor, a struggle which is fraught with all the ambivalence of a love/hate relationship between father and son. The young poet's quest for identity thus takes the form of a ritualized pattern, and the awareness of his indebtedness creates a typically Freudian hostility. The form that the assertion against influence takes, according to Bloom, is the young poet's deliberate misprision, a manipulation of the father's poem, a misinterpretation that is meant to serve as a liberating corrective.

Furthermore, in Bloom's scheme, poetry is everything: religion, art, science are poetic productions. Apparently nothing important is left out of Bloom's system: the production of knowledge is the mechanism of influence, the relation between the texts of fathers and sons. As Frank Lentricchia remarks of Bloom's model, "Literary influence is seen as willful misreading; critical interpretation as willful misreading; even (and this after Freud) life is seen as internecine warfare, one huge demonic 'family romance'" (325). Bloom's scheme can account for everythiing (and indeed is meant to preserve what matters in Western tradition). Though the struggle between fathers and sons is violent, it keeps tradition alive; the contemporary strong poet is engaged against "the death of poetry" (AI 12). No wonder that Bloom writes book after book elaborating his theory; his project is no less than the description of how all knowledge is created and preserved by the mechanism of father/son rivalry.

Yet if Bloom's system seems all-inclusive, we have only to remember that only a few chosen, predominantly male poets are capable, through their battles and misreadings, of preventing "the Death of Poetry." Others cannot escape the mechanism of influence, but are condemned, precisely because they don't acknowledge its power to create weak imitations of their precursors' texts. Using an oedipal analogy, Bloom explains this process: "reject your parents vehemently enough, and you will become a belated version of them, but compound with their reality, and you may partly free yourself" (MM 38). "Reality" here is the divine light of the father that must illuminate the strong poet if he is to be a vehicle of literature's renewal. Those who deny all instructors—his examples of such denigrators of tradition are black poets and women's liberationists—are influenced unconsciously, and their lack of consciousness has grave results. First, they are destined to be but weak versions of those they unconsciously repeat (and so blacks and feminists are unlikely to write good poetry). But even though they are unsuccessful as poets, they can be surprisingly destructive; through blind refusal of their poetic heritage these weak poets have contributed to a loss of our sense of canonical standards.

A poet who is able to correct the past is a good student, always aware of literary tradition as he makes a place for himself in it. The relationship between father and son is described by Bloom as "crucially pedagogical in origin and function":

> You cannot write or teach or think or even read without imitation, and what you imitate is what another person has done, that person's writing, or teaching, or thinking or reading. Your relation to what informs that person is tradition, for tradition is influence that extends past one generation, a carrying-over of influence (*MM* 32).

Bloom's model thus realizes the classic paradigm of pedagogy, of which Jane Gallop says, "The fact that the teacher and student are of the same sex contributes to the interpretation that the student has no otherness, nothing different than the teacher, simply less" (118). In this way, too, his model seems to deny the feminine a place. Because the student always has "less" than the teacher, Bloom can explain the sense of loss and melancholy that he believes characterizes our cultural situation by using the model of an all-powerful father-teacher who makes the son-student feel his belatedness. Poems are increasingly the story of the son's melancholy over his lack of priority. And if this is so, women are not to blame for the threatened position of the contemporary male writer—in fact, women seem to be irrelevant.

A Map of Misreading is Bloom's most explicit expression of what precisely stands to be lost—tradition, canonical standards, poetry itself—and he is correspondingly most adamant in that book about the necessity for instruction and the distinction between "strong" and "weak" poets. But Bloom flounders the more he tries to be clear, and the distinction he wants to maintain ultimately collapses on the issue of the consciousness of the poet. Both the strong and the weak poet are most urgently motivated by the desire to be a great original, according to Bloom. But is the strong poet stronger simply because he is conscious of the tradition, of the need to be original? Here Bloom wavers:

> I greatly prefer Pynchon to Mailer as a writer because a voluntary

parody is more impressive than an involuntary one, but I wonder if our aesthetic possibilities need to be reduced now to just such a choice. Do the dialectics of literary tradition condemn us, at this time, either to an affirmation of belatedness, via Kabbalistic inversion, or to a mock-vitalistic lie-against-time, via an emphasis upon the self-as-performer? I cannot answer this hard question . . . (MM 39).

One wonders if Bloom cannot answer this question because the terms of his choice are not clear, the question not a real one. While emphasizing the "grim" necessity for instruction, for impressing upon the consciousness of the ephebe the importance of the tradition, Bloom also indicates that the weight of this reminder is intolerable: we are in a "cultural situation of such belatedness that literary survival itself seems questionable" (MM 38). Finally, it would seem, a poet cannot function either way. Bloom seems to shrug off this tricky double bind: "Strong students, like strong writers, will find the sustenance they must have" (MM 39). But is this sustenance to be found in conscious reminders of tradition or in the power of the unconscious struggle with one's precursors? In *The Anxiety of Influence*, we learned that the process of becoming a strong poet was primarily an unconscious struggle with one's precursors, and in *A Map of Misreading*, moreover, we learn that the ephebe does not even choose his precursors: "no strong writer can choose his precursors until first he is chosen by them" (MM 39). If the process of becoming a strong poet is necessarily involuntary (he is chosen) and unconscious, the necessity for instruction diminishes. But more importantly, the terms used to make the distinction between the strong poet (the voluntary self-conscious parodist) and the weak (the involuntary unconscious parodist) do not work, and Bloom maintains the distinction only by assertion. The distinction between strong poets and weak poets is the very basis of his explanation for the necessity of tradition. As this crucial distinction and others collapse, the power of assertion becomes even more important precisely because Bloom's defense of tradition is more profoundly at issue than is his explanation of it.

It is revealing that Bloom is so insistent (and arbitrarily assertive) in *A Map of Misreading* at the moment he considers the literature of the "other," blacks and feminists who stand outside the mainstream of the white, male tradition. Bloom obviously wants to protect the continuity of this tradition against a radical disruption by the literature of the other: "I prophesy though that the first true break with literary continuity will be brought about in generations to come, if the burgeoning religion of Liberated Woman spreads from the cluster of enthusiasts to dominate the West" (MM 33). Bloom's "prophecy" carefully contains the power of the Liberated Woman: it belongs now to a "cluster of enthusiasts" who will predominate in the distant future. Yet Bloom's own text reveals that the moment has already arrived and that he is already engaged in the defense against this radical, feminist disruption. Indeed, Bloom's own narrative depends not only upon the confinement but the further repression of woman and the feminine. When stereotypes of the feminine as the site of powerlessness and incoherence fail to protect masculine identity, Bloom effaces the feminine altogether by placing the father in the mother's position. Such strategies are required if Bloom is to protect the integrity of masculine subjectivity.

As Bloom describes it, the tradition we need to preserve is grounded in subjectivity: ". . . the anxiety of influence is strongest where poetry is most lyrical, most subjective, and stemming directly from the personality" (AI 62). Accordingly, Bloom grounds his narration in the psychology of the poet "as poet" and narrates this story as the poet's struggle to attain selfhood, a selfhood that is unique, original, and autonomous. ". . . [A] poet's stance, his Word, his imaginative identity, his whole being, *must* be unique to him, and remain unique, or he will perish, as a poet" (AI 71). In this project, of course, the poet is "doomed" from the start, doomed to discover that "His word is not his word only" (AI 61), that he discovers himself only in relation to others. At such moments in his text, Bloom seems to participate in current notions of intersubjectivity, which tell us that no self is autonomous and discrete. "Derrida has made of writing an intra-psychical trope, which is a making that necessarily pleases any reader who himself has made of influence an intra-psychical trope or rather a trope of intra-poetic relationships" (MM 49). Bloom goes on to emphasize his departure from Derrida: Derrida's Scene of Writing is "insufficiently Primal" (49). But it becomes obvious that Bloom's real disagreement with Derrida is over the loss of a nourishing illusion about the unique and autonomous self. His whole narrative is structured to dramatize the ultimate triumph of this illusion, and so to recuperate and emphasize its value.

Bloom equates this triumphant but illusory autonomy with masculinity: to achieve strong poetic selfhood one must become a man. Bloom cites Kierkegaard to this effect: "He who will not work does

not get the bread but remains deluded, as the gods deluded Orpheus
. . . because he was effeminate, not courageous" (AI 72). Bloom uses
stereotypical figures of the feminine to buttress an opposition of male
and female. The woman is the Sphinx and the Muse who represents
the "natural," "sexual anxiety," and "is met upon the road back to
origins," while the "Covering Cherub" is male and represents "the
human," "creative anxiety," met "upon the road forward to possibility" (AI 36). As muse, woman seems limited in a familiar way; she
is the condition of writing, but not the producer of it.

And yet Bloom's use of these stereotypes grants the feminine a
dangerous power. In the strange Prologue to *The Anxiety of Influence*,
a nameless male persona describes a fall away from fullness that
leaves him silent and wanting to say, "strengthless and female fruit"
(3). The Prologue seems to allude to a pre-oedipal moment when the
mother and pre-verbal infant are located in a symbiotic relationship.
This moment is imaged less passively in Bloom's account of the
Sphinx ("the great Inhibitor" [32] "whose works are mighty" [36]).
The Sphinx, says Bloom, "strangles even strong imaginations in the
cradle" (32). Here the mother represents a terrifying threat to the self.

In the Freudian model, the mother is the enemy of autonomy.
Initially, the child is locked in close symbiotic union with the mother,
and its desire is focused solely upon her. The entry of the father,
embodiment of law and language, into this dualistic structure signals
the beginning of castration anxiety. This anxiety is the terminal crisis
of the oedipal complex in that it has the effect of placing a prohibition
upon the mother as the child's object of desire, precipitating the formation of the superego. We have seen how Lasch accounted for cultural decadence as the weakening of this crucial moment. With the
loss of the father's authority, the superego is weakened; in Freudian
terms, a weak superego is the property of the female, and so men
become feminized. As the oedipal triangle weakens, the mother becomes dominant, threatening male integrity and identity. To protect
the father's authority, male identity (and the oedipal paradigm), John
Irving defends traditional narrative against the rise of woman's authority. For Bloom, as for other writers we have discussed, the mother
is dangerous.

In the first three chapters of *The Anxiety of Influence*, the feminine
is initially present as the overpowering mother—the Sphinx who
strangles even strong imaginations in the cradle—or the Muse, who
is the ephebe's "beloved." But just as it is essential to the individu-
ation of the child to separate from the mother, so it is for the young

ephebe: "The longer he dwells with her, the smaller he becomes, as though he proved man only by exhaustion" (AI 61). The logic of this Freudian account requires the repression of the mother. Yet for Bloom, even acknowledging this need for repression grants the feminine too much power. After discussing how language to some degree compensates the child for, as Bloom puts it, "maternal abandonment," Bloom in turn abandons the mother. The last three chapters of *The Anxiety of Influence* further repress the feminine by dramatizing the internalization and the repression, not of the mother, but of the precursor father. In Bloom's account, the precursor father is made to represent the important threat to the poet's loss of self. Bloom's double repression of the feminine represents his own revisionary swerve from the Freudian model of the oedipal complex.

Yet in order to make this substitution work, Bloom must imply that the oedipal complex is never successfully completed for the young ephebe:

> Freud humanely saw the Oedipus complex as only a phase in the development of character, to be superseded by the *überich* (superego) as mock rational censor. Yet no poet-as-poet completes such development and still remains a poet. In the imagination, the Oedipal phase *develops backwards*, to enrich . . . the id (AI 109–10).

The poetic father, in other words, is absorbed not into the superego, as he would be in normal development, but into the id. In this regressive movement, repression is augmented—"every forgotten precursor becomes a giant in the imagination" (AI 107)—and the precursor's text is substituted for the mother's body as the scene of separation. In place of the taboo against incest with the mother, Bloom substitutes a taboo against incest with the precursor-father. By the time Bloom tells us that poetry is the "enchantment of incest, disciplined by the resistance to that enchantment" (AI 95), incest has come to look like a homosexual attachment to the father.

Bloom follows the Freudian scheme, then, in acknowledging the importance of repression in the formation of identity, but in Bloom's scheme, the poet must resist or repress his desire for incest with the father rather than the mother. The mother is doubly repressed in Bloom's account, for he substitutes the place of the father for the place of the mother. Why is it important for him to discuss separation in terms of the father rather than the mother? Since the son becomes the father, Bloom is able to explain the loss of autonomy in relation to the father while still holding out the promise, however illusory, that the son's autonomy in the form of poetic identity can still be recuperated. In contrast, the son's relationship to the mother only promises an annhilation of the self.

Despite his focus upon the father as the source of the poet's creative anxiety, the metaphors that Bloom uses to describe what threatens the poet and poetry-making reveal that the mother's position is a radical threat to subjectivity and hence an even more powerful source of anxiety. In other words, Bloom's thesis seems to be that poetry-making is the story of a struggle between fathers and sons. But by looking at the way images of the feminine operate in his text, we can see that the feminine is more essential to the process of poetry making that Bloom explicitly admits. For instance, he describes anxiety this way: "the anxiety of influence is an anxiety in expectation of *being flooded*" (AI 57, his italics). His texts on anxiety are awash in images of the flood, the sea, an "oceanic sense" (MM 11). A Stevens poem, to give one instance, is described as recounting "a fearful vision"; it "is Whitman's terrible mother let loose upon the land . . . 'an un-named flowing'—of 'the river that flows nowhere' like a sea" (MM 20). Bloom explicitly connects this flooding and the anxiety of influence to Freud's account of the birth trauma and the fear of being trapped in the Mother (AI 57). A secondary source of anxiety, Bloom reminds us, is caused by separation from the mother . . . though this separation is typically described in Bloom's text as "falling," not explicitly from the all-encompassing mother but from God: "Poetry begins with our awareness, not of a Fall, but that *we are falling*" (AI 20). If we return again to the Prologue to *The Anxiety of Influence*, we can see that its language of "Fullness," "silence," the desire to say "strengthless and female fruit" (3) image the feminine as an absolute fullness and as an absolute depletion: both make speech impossible.

Bloom attempts to defend himself against this version of femininity and the threat it poses to speech in a number of ways. First, like his ephebes, he must prove his masculinity. Thus the exaggeratedly masculine voice: he is a tough guy doing a dirty job. "Poets-as-poets are not lovable and critics have been slow to know this, which is why criticism has not yet turned to its rightful function: the study and problematics of loss" (MM 18). Second, his effort to defend himself against a seemingly feminine lack of definition leads him to erect rigid systems—maps, stereotypic oppositions, a highly ritualized pattern of literary genealogy. But if the feminine represents a loss of ability to make distinctions and to map clear boundaries, then Bloom's own text reveals that his stridently masculine voice and defensive strategies are an inadequate barrier against the flood.

A good example of how he fails to make himself plain, or even intelligible, occurs in his discussion of the Covering Cherub, an emblematic figure for the poet's creative and/or potentially crippling anxiety. This point in the text would seem to be a crucial one of definition and distinction, yet Bloom begins with an apparently inexhaustible list of analogies: "Milton was the Tyger, the Covering Cherub blocking a new voice from entering the Poet's Paradise. The emblem of this discussion is the Covering Cherub. In Genesis he is God's Angel; in Ezekiel he is the Prince of Tyre; in Blake he is fallen Tharmas, and the Spector of Milton; in Yeats he is the Spectre of Blake" (AI 35). Then he admits that an exhaustive summary of the Cherub's incarnations is impossible: ". . . he is a poor demon of many names (as many names as there are strong poets) but I summon him first namelessly, as a final name is not yet devised by men for the anxiety that blocks their creativeness" (AI 35). In devising this catalog of names for the nameless, Bloom, out of control, spins an open-ended catalog. Discussing the ephebe's creative process, Bloom later holds that his mode of signification, an endless chain of substitutes, is grounded in the ephebe's loss of the Mother-Muse. The poet "overestimates" the "Muse, seeing her as unique and irreplaceable, for how else can he be assured that *he* [his italics] is unique and irreplaceable? Freud dryly remarks that the pressing desire in the unconscious for some irreplaceable thing often resolves itself into an endless series in actuality" (AI 63).

Such assertions suggest that Freud and Bloom have everything under control. They can identify what is lost, which is nothing more than an overrated woman, the mother. But we should recall that in this discussion of the Covering Cherub, Bloom is intent upon positioning the ephebe in relationship to the *father*. The Covering Cherub is initially referred to as "he," but Bloom's analogies begin to spill over the boundary that separates masculinity and femininity. He writes: "The Covering Cherub may masquerade as the Sphinx . . . but the Sphinx (whose works are mighty) must be a female (or at least a female male). The Cherub is male (or at least a male female)" (AI 36). In this incoherent merging of categories one sees the hysteric's attempt simultaneously to maintain and to resist sexual identity.

Bloom's bewildering analogies and distinctions are followed by spatial images that paradoxically make it even harder to locate where we are. First, the Covering Cherub "only covers, he only appears to block the way" (AI 36). The Cherub covers "everything that nature itself covers; in Ezekiel, the richness of the earth, but by the Blakean paradox of *appearing to be those riches*; in Genesis, the Eastern Gate, the way to the Tree of Life." But then, "the Covering Cherub stands between the achieved Man . . . and the emanation or beloved" (AI 38). "The Covering Cherub separates, then?" (38). "No," we learn that "he has no power to do so" (38) but is a "demon of continuity; his baleful charm imprisons the present in the past, and reduces a world of differences into a grayness of uniformity" (AI 39).

Such a demon has obviously infected Bloom's own style of representation. Here and elsewhere Bloom substitutes for analysis a confusing chain of analogies, which, in effect, insists that everything is the same as everything else. So, of course, he fails to preserve the sexual differences he so adamantly desires. Who is ultimately responsible for the loss of autonomy, and therefore the anxiety of influence? The overpowering mother or the overpowering father? Even Bloom's prologue, which narrates a fall into "strengthless and female fruit," is entitled "It Was A Great Marvel That They Were In The Father Without Knowing Him." Bloom's shifts indicate his own inability to position male and female precisely, though he desperately wants to.

What is at stake in this sort of positioning is an assured autonomy and identity that Bloom wants both for his poets and for himself. Autonomous selfhood depends upon separating masculinity and femininity into distinct realms, on banishing otherness. And this desire for autonomy, for establishing difference, is at work, too, for those feminist critics intent upon the positioning of the woman writer. Several of these critics, notably Gilbert and Gubar in *The Madwoman in the Attic,* have incorporated Bloom's theory of influence to describe the woman writer's relation to male precursors and to stress the equal importance of female precursors. Accepting Bloom's story as "right (or at least suggestive)" (47), rather than scrutinizing it for inconsistencies, these feminists ask the question: how might the process of influence differ for women writers?

Demonstrating in a convincing and thorough way the debilitating anxieties imposed upon women writers in the nineteenth century by a patriarchal literary tradition, Gilbert and Gubar assert that women write under a condition of doubleness apparently not shared by men. The woman writer must respond to both her femininity and to oppressive male misreadings of women. Turning away from the anxieties of women writers, Gilbert and Gubar begin to deemphasize the woman writer's relation to the father and to stress the importance of a powerful but finally benign mother, just as Bloom represses the threatening mother in order to focus upon the poet's relationship to the threatening but less overwhelming father. Both Bloom, in his defense of a male line of continuity and influence, and Gilbert and Gubar, in their advocacy of a female line of continuity and influence, undertake a nostalgic search for origins, a quest that is informed by a sense of loss and motivated by the desire for self-definition and wholeness. "Yearning for [a] lost female home," (just as they claim their women writers did), Gilbert and Gubar write that:

> this book is a dream of the rising of Christina Rosetti's "mother country." And there is a sense in which it is an attempt at reconstructing the Sibyl's leaves, leaves which haunt us with the possibility that if we can piece together the fragments the parts will form a whole that tells the story of the career of a single woman artist, a "mother of us all" . . . (102).

Just as Bloom intends to preserve the nourishing illusion of male autonomy and subjectivity, so Gilbert and Gubar dream of emerging with a vision of the woman artist, made "whole" and "energetic" through a nourishing relationship to her mythical maternal origins. Both accounts, while giving glancing acknowledgment to self-division and repression, insist finally upon psychic integrity and sexual difference.

The purpose of our analysis has been to show that this tenacious insistence upon integrity and difference can only be tentatively maintained. Bloom too writes under a condition of doubleness, a condition that he would deny and repress, but that finally introduces incoherence, gaps, and contradictions into his text and compromises his pose as a tough, masculine critic able to construct a coherent model based upon oppositions. We are suggesting that a more fruitful feminist reading would articulate the operation of difference and tension *within* a discourse rather than set up the difference and tension *between* male and female discourses. Explicitly, this project would be informed by the post-structuralist perspective suggested but ultimately denied in Bloom's text. As Lentricchia points out, Bloom's debate with Derrida is "misguided," for "the preponderance of evidence from his texts demonstrates that 'eloquence' is no more than an intertextual phenomenon, a scene of writing, a play of differences, not the product of a primal scene of instruction or of a gigantic imperial will" (344). We would agree with Lentricchia, but our analysis demonstrates that Bloom needs to resist these implications in order to preserve sexual difference and identity. As do the other nostalgic writers we discuss, Bloom associates the marks of postmodernist writing, its decentered play that deconstructs oppositions, grounding principles, and integrity, with the feminization of writing and authority. Bloom both acknowledges and forcefully represses the marks of this writing. His implicit participation in the feminization of authority, distressing as it is, might perhaps give us hope: Bloom's "liberated woman" is already shaking the edifice of masculine textuality—from within it.

Chapter
Five

Feminist
Scholarship
as
Shadow
Work

For more than a decade, Ivan Illich has offered a bleak description of the losses suffered by men and women as a result of the transformation brought about by capitalism and economic growth. In his books, he describes how physical and emotional resources necessary to nurture any gratifying life have been transferred to care-giving institutions that not only thrive on transforming these once accessible resources into scarce commodities but also alienate themselves from the best interests of the very people they are meant to serve. Like the other writers we have discussed (he even refers the reader to the work of Lasch and the Bergers), Illich reports on a degenerate present and mourns what we have lost. In his latest book, *Gender*, Illich broadens his familiar thesis to insist that there is a "gender-specific pain of loss" under this "*new* experience of economic misery": women suffer more than men (175). His purpose is, as he puts it, to "listen more attentively to the report of the losers," who are still suffering despite the feminist struggle for equal rights and better jobs (178).

Feminists have hardly been grateful to Illich for his "attentive" report. After listening to him present his theory of gender during a Regents' lecture series at Berkeley, several feminists organized a symposium to critique his work. Their critiques, employing a wide variety of approaches—anthropological, linguistic, economic—were published in *Feminist Issues.* The consensus was that *Gender* is reactionary, unintelligible propaganda. Arlie Hochschild perceives Illich's "sad" message to be ". . . that women have no place in the modern world; that equality with men is impossible for most of us; and that men have no place in the heartland of the home." "Once this message is clearly perceived," Hochschild expects that "it will get the reception it deserves" (11).

But by choosing to greet Illich with denunciation and dismissal, we would close off an important line of inquiry. Illich relies heavily upon feminist scholarship to support his claim that life in the distant past was better for both sexes, but particularly for women. The ease with which Illich appropriates a wealth of feminist scholarship to this end prompts our inquiry into those feminist analyses of woman's culture that locate and praise a distinctly feminine identity. Illich, too, is in the business of promoting the importance of women's difference from men. Is Illich's nostalgia reinforced by a nostalgic trend in women's studies?

Our second, and related purpose, is to analyze Illich's textual strategies. There is a complex relationship between Illich's text and the feminist scholarship he relies upon. In those places where *Gender* relies on feminist scholarship the most, the notes expand so much that his own text nearly disappears. Indeed, it is almost impossible to say that there is an Illich "text" *per se,* or an autonomous message, an isolated stance; Illich's book, as even a simple glance indicates, is a graphic example of intertextuality. In other words, Illich draws upon a multiplicity of scholarly texts in order to construct the "reality" of what we have lost, a vernacular culture. Some of these texts he has written himself. On page 16 of *Gender* for example, he quotes himself four times. This condition of textuality puts him in a bind, for as Eugene Vance has pointed out, "the more [the text] participates in an order of discourse, the less its signifiers point to some expressive or referential context: they point, instead, only to the discourse in which they begin and end" (49). Caught up in, and dispossessed by a centerless, never-ending productivity that is properly textual, Illich displays his anxiety over the absence of any certain access to the referent by yearning for a stable referential text—his own, one that will not just be distinct from others, but clearer, realer, closer to the truth. We will demonstrate, then, how his nostalgia for subsistence rather than economy, for authentic gender-bound behavior, for a purer language that would give us more direct access to this world, is motivated by a desire for a stable referent, that is, a fixed point, a center which orders everything around it, and by which all things are measured. Illich mourns the loss of a fictional realm of his own creation, and yet he is intent upon naturalizing it as a fundamental reality. This "reality" acts in his text as an "authentic" origin or center from which to measure the more "degenerate" present.

We will begin, then, by discussing how Illich creates this "purer" past by appropriating a certain kind of feminist scholarship. Two topics that have engaged feminist scholars are of particular interest to Illich: the status of women in precapitalist society and the transformation of their position as a result of the onset of capitalism. Work on these topics is important to Illich, since in *Gender* he is describing a transformation from what he calls a "vernacular" culture, that is, a "traditional" culture located in the distant past in which each gender had its own distinct perceptions, behavior, tools, and speech, to an economic and sexist culture in which men and women have lost their primordial sense of their separate identities. Illich tells us that economic growth is the key to this transformation, in other words, the key to what he considers women's "gender-specific sense of loss" (175). He devotes the first half of his book to describing how this is so.

Relying heavily upon feminist studies to document his claims, Illich elucidates the discrimination against women in three areas: the public sector, what he calls the reported economy, where "the median yearly earnings of the average full-time employed woman still hovers around a magical ratio (3:5) of a man's average earnings" (24); the unreported economy where there is no legally recognized salary and so equal opportunity laws do not apply to protect such women workers as prostitutes, or typists and babysitters who work at home; and finally, the area he calls "shadow work," the "unpaid toil that adds to a commodity an incremental value that is necessary to make this commodity useful to the consuming unit" (45). Illich finds this sector to be the most discriminatory against women. With economic growth and the increase of wage labor, the submerged drudgery that keeps that economy floating must expand. Housework is his paradigmatic example of that sort of drudgery. Curiously, much of what Illich says here depends on feminist scholarship and if he did not lack a sense of irony, he would see how he is converting that scholarship itself into shadow work.

In the process of articulating his concept of shadow work, Illich mentions in his footnotes the work of Gisela Bock and Barbara Duden, Ann Oakley, Susan Strasser, Sarah Fenstermaker Berk, to mention a few. In these footnotes he is generous; their work is "fun to read and superbly organized," or "lively" and "crammed with precise information," and so forth (47). But it appears he can only be generous when he is not too dependent. His use of Heidi Hartmann's work illuminates his characteristic strategies of appropriation.

When Illich discusses housework, he makes no mention of Hartmann, whose article "The Family as the Locus of Gender, Class, and Political Struggle: The Example of Housework," he effectively obscures by citing several pages back in a footnote entitled "Reproduction" (35–36). In this way, Illich attempts to hide her work by not citing it at the appropriate moment, and to subsume her work under the aegis of another topic, "reproduction," that he then scornfully dismisses. Illich does not like the word *reproduction*, which to him signifies a degendered, mechanical process of duplication, like Xeroxing. Postwar feminists, he tells us, borrowing from male theorists like "Marx, Reich, and Freud," in order to gain legitimacy, learned to use the word "reproduction." Theories of reproduction "crop up like weeds" in the writings of North American feminists. Using words like "production" and "reproduction," these feminists made "women's rights and workers' rights seem compatible with industrial development and progress" (Illich 35–36). In other words, the feminists' confused attempt to apply borrowed words resulted in obscuring the reality Illich hopes he has just made sparklingly clear: that industrial development makes things worse, not better, for women. In fact, of course, this argument is not different from but parallel to the work of women scholars who long ago noted discrimination against women in industrial society. In this respect, the only gesture of acknowledgment Illich makes is an extremely backhanded compliment: "In spite of its weakness and dullness, this research remains fundamental for our understanding of how industrial society works" (35). Hartmann's work is cited as "far above average" but still denigrated because representative of the trend in women's studies mistaking the importance of words like "production and reproduction" (35).

Just how fundamental Hartmann actually is to Illich's work can be seen by looking specifically at the way both discuss housework. Here is how Hartmann discusses it:

> With the wages they receive, people buy the commodities that they need for their survival. Once in the home these commodities are then transformed to become usable in producing and reproducing people. In our society, which is organized by patriarchy as well as by capitalism, the sexual division of labor by gender makes men primarily responsible for wage labor and women primarily responsible for household production. That portion of household production called housework consists largely in purchasing commodities and transforming them into usuable forms. Sheets, for example, must be bought, put on beds, rearranged after every sleep, and washed, just as food must be bought, cleaned, cooked, and served to become a meal (372–73).

And this is how Illich talks about shadow work, specifically housework:

> Unlike the production of goods and services, shadow work is performed by the consumer of commodities, specifically, the consuming household. I call shadow work any *labor* by which the consumer transforms a purchased commodity into a usable good. I designate as shadow work the time, toil, and effort that must be expended in order to add to any purchased commodity the value without which it is unfit for use. Therefore, shadow work names an activity in which people must engage to whatever degree they attempt to satisfy their needs by means of commodities. By introducing the term "shadow work," I distinguish the procedure for cooking eggs today from that followed in the past. When a modern housewife goes to the market, picks up the eggs, drives them home in her car, takes the elevator to the seventh floor, turns on the stove, takes butter from the refrigerator, and fries the eggs, she adds value to the commodity with each one of these steps. This is not what her grandmother did. The latter looked for eggs in the chicken coop, cut a piece from the lard she had rendered, lit some wood her kids had gathered on the commons, and added the salt she had bought. Although

101

this example might sound romantic, it should make the economic difference clear. Both women prepare fried eggs, but only one uses a marketed commodity and highly capitalized production goods: car, elevator, electric appliances. The grandmother carries out woman's gender-specific tasks in creating subsistence; the new housewife must put up with the household burden of shadow work (48–49).

Hartmann says, "Housework consists largely in purchasing commodities and transforming them into usable forms." Illich says, "I call shadow work any labor by which the consumer transforms a purchased commodity into a usable good." The parallels continue. Hartmann's argument determines the shape of Illich's text, which follows her argument by providing an example of housework. His only original contribution is a new name for housework, "shadow work."

What does Illich gain by changing the language used? By dismissing the word "reproduction," he can insist that he is giving us a purer, fundamentally clearer picture of reality. His insistence upon the word "shadow work," rather than "housework," operates in a similar way. In the late nineteenth and early twentieth centuries, there was an optimistic hope, expressed by Charlotte Gilman and others, that capitalism and technology would free woman of the burden of housework. The question Hartmann and others pose is why, when women have jobs, as well as more technology at their disposal, is housework still considered women's domain? Using the term "shadow work," Illich neutralizes what most women still perceive to be a gendered task—housework—thus creating by his act of naming a neutered domain. By his act of naming, Illich creates the problem he wants to talk about, that is, the problem of a "unisex" world. He does this in his example of housework too, which echoes yet oddly skews Hartmann's example. Where Hartmann's example is hardly nostalgic, Illich's is deliberately romanticized to make the past seem better because more sharply gendered. Here again, Illich is engaged in creating the myth of a neutered present as a way of decrying a loss of difference. Grandma's work was gendered, while the modern housewife's is not. What may seem confusing about this is that the pronouns Illich uses indicate that the modern housewife is clearly a woman, as, obviously, is her grandmother, so it is hard to figure out how housework has become less "shaped by gender" (to use Illich's phrase) than it was in the past.

A quick review of Illich's use of feminist scholarship should begin to indicate what really bothers Illich about the "unisex world" of the present. Illich's tactics involve mustering up statistics, mostly provided by women scholars, to support his claim that the present is hardly fair to women—they are still economically oppressed (oppressed by economics is how Illich would put it). But he twists these studies to his own purposes. While Hartmann and others ask why housework is still women's domain, Illich worries that it is becoming *less* women's domain: "With every year that passes, shadow work becomes more obviously genderless . . . Now, with more men being forced into shadow work as employment becomes ever more scarce, discrimination against women, right in their homes, will become more pronounced" (59). In other words, men are moving into women's domain, women's position, while women (and this is what bothers Illich) are moving into men's. Women are becoming scholars and writers, for instance. Illich reveals his anxieties about this change in position by denigrating, in order to master, the very feminist scholarship upon which he relies. It is his sense of the loss of male certainty and prerogatives, particularly the male prerogative over the power of writing and scholarship, which prompts his passionate tract. Illich would like to persuade women that it is in their best interest to preserve the power of their domain, the kitchen. But his overt polemical purpose only thinly disguises a more urgent one: to preserve *men's* domain and authority.

Illich is particularly insidious when he relies upon women scholars who themselves promote the importance of sexual difference by advocating the value of separate domains. Much of his material comes from anthropological studies, but here too he must present the material in such a way as to seem to have a superior grasp of its implications. He does this by again insisting upon the importance of changing the language of these studies: his own "purified" language will bring us closer to reality and the truth.

In a subchapter entitled "Social Science Sexism," Illich describes how anthropologists in the 1930s made important observations about "gender-bound behavior" the significance of which they could not understand. The term "sex-role" was a particular obstacle: "Role is the device by which people become part of a plural that can then be analyzed by genderless concepts" (80). Illich, who tells us that the word "role" comes from theater, wants us to understand that using the term *role* perpetuates a distance from authentic reality. Male anthropologists, he says, used the language of sex role, defining gendered behavior in a way that made this behavior seem malleable. Later, "around the middle of the century" (87), these anthropologists in the pay of economic policy makers could cast gender-bound behavior as "sex-role stereotypes" that were then simply seen as a barrier to economic progress. In the early seventies, when feminists tried to correct the male bias of the discipline and record the activities of women, they were kept at a distance from the experience they were examining, hindered by the inadequacies of the language of sex roles, inherited from their male predecessors. As a result, says Illich, "women's studies have acted as a further camouflage of gender" (89). In other words, the use of a male-biased language deprived women of the power to understand the meaning of their own research, and once again, obscured reality. Such a criticism would lead us to expect that Illich has independent observations to offer. But in fact his interpretation of modernization and the life that preceded it relies heavily on feminist anthropological studies.

One book Illich cites is Esther Boserup's important *Women's Role in Economic Development* (1974), which delineates the negative effects that colonialism and the penetration of capitalism into subsistence economies have often had on women. Boserup's findings were obviously crucial to Illich's own arguments about the negative effects of economic growth on women; he cites as well the other works by feminists which have both refined and expanded upon Boserup's study. Boserup also pointed out that previous anthropological studies were ideologically biased toward the undervaluation of women's work and neglected their participation in economic life. Several studies following Boserup's and cited by Illich are devoted to two points: the importance of women's activities in precapitalist, subsistence communities, and the loss of their status and power under economic growth.

In Mona Etienne and Eleanor Leacock's anthology, *Women and Colonization*, for example, several cultures are described as they were before and after the invasion of capitalism and the imposition of a European, male-biased culture. The cultures described are structured in diverse ways, but the primary purpose of the anthology is to demonstrate the "reality of female-male complementarity" that existed in these societies. That is, women had spheres of power and activity that were different from but equally as important as those areas controlled by men; the two sexes were interdependent. In *Women and Colonization*, complementarity between the sexes is crucially linked to a subsistence, or precapitalist, economy. It is best demonstrated by "hunting and gathering" tribes, which we are told were egalitarian. There was seemingly a direct and equal participation of all adults in the production of basic necessities; people made decisions about activities for which they were responsible, the division of labor was by sex only, and relations were reciprocal (Etienne and Leacock 9). Clearly, the contrast Leacock and Etienne are drawing is between the "separate but equal" spheres of these societies, and the separate but unequal spheres of capitalist societies. According to Etienne and Leacock, "a male 'public' domain and a female 'private' domain can be clearly dissociated only after stratification and privatization of women's productive and reproductive capacity has occurred" (5). In other words, the economic system, especially capitalism, creates inequality. Separate sexual spheres, that is, sexual difference, is not fundamentally a problem; indeed, focusing on women's activities and their sources of power and status often leads to a valorizing of those spheres.

In another study, "History, Development, and the Division of Labor by Sex: Implications for Organization," Leacock holds up the Warribri women as a model for feminist action because "they are not fighting to achieve a status they have never held by breaking into areas defined as male. Instead, they are fighting to protect and enhance the domain that once assured their security and independence" (488). An insistence on separate spheres is also crucial to an article entitled "The Position of Women: Appearance and Reality" by Ernestine Friedl that Illich cites three times. (He calls it "delightful.") Friedl sets out to demonstrate that the "appearance" of male prestige in Greek culture disguises the "reality" of women's power. Friedl simply reverses the value attached to women's sphere so as to valorize what is typically undervalued: "women in a Greek village hold a position of real power in the life of the family and the life of the family is the most significant structural and cultural element of the Greek village" (97).

By focusing upon a woman's sphere of activity, and insisting upon her power within this sphere, some women scholars in anthropology are attempting to refute both the claim of "universal female subordination," an important debate which Illich barely acknowledges, and the sociobiological claim of women's natural inferiority. Nevertheless, Illich is able to make use of this current focus upon "women's sphere"—her activities, status, ultimately her important (even valorized) difference—because he too is in the business of promoting sexual difference. His portrait of vernacular culture depends upon

105

setting up distinct spheres of men and women as well as a subsistence culture where men and women are in direct relationship to each other, to the decision-making process, and to the goods they produce and consume. A certain trend in anthropological feminist scholarship, a trend that also emphasizes sexual difference and women's happier life in a subsistence culture, informs his book and suits his purposes.

Of course, the assumption of sexual difference and the attitudes toward language and self that it entails are basic to the discussion of women's culture in many fields. In fact, the assumption is basic to the field of women's studies itself. As Hester Eisenstein has remarked:

> . . . Women's Studies researchers set out to uncover and to document the worlds of women, and to begin the work of describing and analyzing women's history, psychology, anthropology, and literature, among other areas . . . When feminist writers were rediscovering sex roles and demonstrating their uses in the perpetuation of patriarchy, they had stressed the need to abolish culturally produced differences between women and men as the surest path to equality. Now, far from seeking to minimize women's differences from men, feminist scholars were asserting their importance as a legitimate and even a crucial focus of study.
>
> This focus upon women—what Gerda Lerner has called a "woman-centered analysis"—gradually produced a change in attitude toward the value of women's differences from men. Originally seen as a source of oppression, these were now beginning to appear, on the contrary, as a source of enrichment (xviii).

The danger in seeing women's difference as a source of "enrichment" is precisely that a sphere that is essentially an ideological construct (a construct formerly perceived to be oppressive) begins to slip into a sphere that is perceived to be "reality."[1] Some anthropologists have sought out this sphere in order to describe women's status in other cultures. The assumption informing this search is that though women's activities may have been observed, no one has talked to women to get the "real" account of their lives, or seen the importance of their activities. In many ways this assumption is sensible. Women have long been relegated to the margins of discourse or to silence. But getting to the "truth" of female experience is more difficult than these accounts acknowledge.

Women must make certain assumptions about the self and the transparency of language in order to get to the "truth" in this way. Often, they must assume that the female informant has an essential self that only she can know. If the informant says she is not subordinate to men, you should believe her story. But a simple acceptance of this statement (or of Illich's statements, for that matter) does not allow reflection on the complexity of the language systems in which we find ourselves. Neither women nor men have complete autonomy from larger social structures that may be guiding their lives and speech. Anthropologists, too, lack autonomy, their reports mediating between the informant and the reader. As a result, the female informant's self is never fully represented in a speech whose meaning is clearly revealed by the anthropologist. As Teresa De Lauretis reminds us, "The relation between women as historical subjects and the notion of woman as it is produced by hegemonic discourses is neither a direct relation of identity, a one-to-one correspondence, nor a relation of simple identification. Like all other relations expressed in language, it is an arbitrary and symbolic one, that is to say, culturally set up" (5–6). To get at the relation between "women" and "woman," we must both listen to what women have to say about their lives *and* we must consider how these statements engage and resist the powerful discursive systems that have so long attempted to naturalize the place of "woman."

Illich insists, in an extreme way, upon spheres that are separate, autonomous, and privileged. Speaking of the home in that golden past, for example, he writes: "In vernacular culture, dwelling and living coincide. With gender-bound tools, oriented by a gender-specific meaning, vernacular life weaves a gendered cocoon set in a biological niche" (119). If this past was so right and natural for women, what must they suffer in the present? Illich explains: "The encroachment and usurpation of normative space frustrates the flesh of women as it does not and could not affect men's . . . Their potential contribution to homemaking is frustrated, and they are yanked out of their proper gender context; it both respects, they suffer more than men" (122). No contemporary feminist is likely to complain that her flesh creeps at the very idea of a man doing the dishes in her kitchen, but Illich's text demonstrates the polemical uses to which discussion of separate but balanced and complementary spheres can be put.

Here an emphasis on separate spheres becomes an insistence upon opposition, wherein one term becomes a referent of the other, producing hierarchy. Illich tries to evade this hierarchy by describing

107

these spheres not as opposed, but as "asymmetrical." He uses the term "asymmetrical" because he understands that oppositions often function to make one term a referent for the other, and he does not want to create a set of dualities dependent on each other for their meaning. His insistence on the cataclysmic division between the past and the present is one way of avoiding such a trap. "I have tried," Illich tells us, ". . . to bring into view the chasm that divides present from the past" (177). The past, in other words, is so radically other that we can not begin to compare it to the present. But if the past is truly so different from the present and its means of articulation, how is he to evoke it for us? He must somehow retrieve what is lost so that we can feel this loss as acutely as he does.

To this end, he adopts two strategies: he adopts a poetic language and employs a process of redefinition that creates a new language. Unfortunately, in his few attempts to render the past in poetic language, he lapses into incoherence. For example, Illich tells us that "the matrix of sex [sex is linked with the present] is Alma Mater; the matrix of gender [gender is associated with the past] can only be found beyond 'the cavern of the seven sleepers,' 'lodged in rock-clefts on the branches of enormous hollow yews'" (177). Since this is not exactly precise (or even very evocative), Illich relies far more heavily upon creating a new language in which old words are redefined and new words adopted. He must purge language of words that bear an accumulated freight of associations that "blur" or "camouflage" reality (we have seen how he attempts to do this with words like "sex role" and "reproduction," for example). Finally, in his text, the desire for clear reference and for a clear referent overwhelms his attempt to create what he calls "delicate asymmetrical" relationships. We can further see this desire for clear reference in his compulsion to maintain distinctions. His scholarship is to be distinguished from women's studies scholarship; the organizing principle for the book itself, the mechanism for dividing past and present, is maintained by yet more distinctions: reality vs. appearance, autonomy vs. control, public vs. private, vernacular tongue vs. taught mother tongue, gender vs. sex. Ultimately, these "distinctions" are set in opposition, not only explaining each other, but producing a privileged referent. We can only understand what we don't have in the present, the "industrial age and its chimeras" by reference to the more substantial reality of the past (21). His scholarship is privileged over the insubstantial scholarship of women and will in fact dispel their confusion: "my distinction between gender and sex . . . could dispel much of the confusion so far inevitable when the 'subordination of women' is discussed" (89). He has, in other words, relegated supposedly asymmetrically balanced differences and distinctions into a hierarchical arrangement of explanation and opposition.

We are now in a better position to see how the desires for difference and for a subsistence culture are related. The past is not simply different from, but better than, the present. And correspondingly, *women's place* in the past was not simply different from, but better than it is in the present, because within this realm women experienced both a power and authority they now have lost. Illich relies upon women's scholarship that valorizes women's sphere; he also exploits the nostalgia implicit in several of these feminist accounts that describe women's sphere as a product of a precapitalist or subsistence culture. As Illich puts it: "subsistence economy coincides with gendered existence" (94). The *desire* for both coincide, we would say, because both are nostalgic, not simply in locating an authentic difference and a subsistence economy in the past, but because the desire for a subsistence culture, like the desire for an authentic difference, reveals a desire for a stable referent.

In Illich's account, capitalism is sometimes the cause for the loss of gender, and sometimes the effect. In the opening pages of *Gender*, capitalism is the effect: ". . . the loss of vernacular gender is the decisive condition for the rise of capitalism" (Illich 3). Yet, a few pages later, capitalism is the cause: "All economic growth entails the destruction of *vernacular gender*" (5). We get the idea that capitalism, or economic growth, as Illich puts it, is a fundamental problem, but his text reveals that it disintegrates as an adequate historical explanation in the traditional sense. We can, however, see what subsistence and capitalism represent to Illich. Subsistence culture is a culture in which people have direct access and are in direct relationship to meaning: the meaning of who they are, what they do, the words they speak. "Kinship" in these cultures, Illich tells us, "organizes the rules of who is who to whom . . ." and "gender not only tells who is who, but it also defines who is when, where, and with which tools and words" (99). There is, moreover, an origin for this meaning in the home: "'Vernacular' means those things that are homemade, homespun, home-grown, not destined for marketplace, but that are for home use only" (68). [Illich does not point out that *vernacular* derives from the word "verna," which means "slave born in the house."] In capitalism, on the other hand, we no longer have privileged access to the authentic truth and meaning about ourselves: "The paradigm of Homo-oeconomicus," that is, women and men under economic growth, "does not square with what men and women actually are" (66).

Capitalism depends, not upon direct exchange and direct relationships to meaning, but upon the creation of surplus whose value is determined within a system of an abstract means of exchange, money. "Historically," Illich tells us, "the regime of scarcity was introduced through the proliferation of money as a scarce means of exchange . . ." (19). Money proliferates, but it is scarce—Illich does not offer a detailed economic or class analysis of the relationship at work here; what seems more important to him is the connotations of the word *scarcity*, which suggests the poverty of the present as compared with the plenitude of the past. But as Eugene Vance has pointed out, the proliferation of money, its increased use as a means of exchange as well as a source of profit, is precisely bound up in the same problematic as the proliferation of the printed word, the text.

We can use Vance's discussion of medieval poetry to explain how the story of the losses brought about by a money economy is a story about language as well, a relation crucial for Illich, but one that he never examines. According to Vance, the development of a "new economics" based on the circulation of money disturbed a "Christian ethics of transparence" in which words were provided a clear and stable referent through God's act of naming the world. This ethics of transparence was promoted by the Church fathers in what Vance calls the "arch-culture of Latinity." In this culture, all texts gained their truth in relation to the founding truth of the divine father (Vance 41–42).[2] In an effort to appropriate some of this authority for himself, Illich uses Latin as the language of truth. So, for example, the *gens* and the *lars* identify the realms of men and women, while today the genderless individual is a "rapacious neutrum oeconomicum" (Illich 179).[3] Illich's use of Latin insists on the founding truth of the father and reminds us that the "ethics of transparency" was (and is) not neutral because it awards the male voice privileged authority through its access to the father's truth. There are echoes of this privilege not only in Illich's use of Latin but also in the way he describes male and female language within a vernacular culture. Men have "straight speech," a language of immediacy and presence, and women, according to Illich, are given the voice of "whisperings and gossip" (113).

In the Middle Ages, the notion of language as bound to a stable referent was disturbed by the increased circulation of money and texts. Money, says Vance, became "endowed with special powers of abstraction . . . and functioned independently of origins in men . . . the 'referentiality' of a piece of money was only the system of currency itself" (44). Moreover, money began regularly generating profit from money, giving rise to the practice of usury, which the clergy condemned. It is precisely this homology between the productivity of money in capitalism, and the productivity of texts, which Eugene Vance stresses:

> Finally, just as the circulation of money gave rise to a productivity that was strictly monetary (usury), so too the errant text would compel, in its displacements and translations, the production, out of nothing, of other displaceable texts. In such a process, which others have called "intertextuality," the meaning of specific texts was no longer to be found elsewhere than in the sheer productivity of writing itself, in textuality as a kind of fetishism which sustained itself only because it constantly displaced "meaning" with each instance of renewal (46).

He later adds, ". . . the signifiers with which [the medieval poet] names either his desire or the object of his desire originate neither within the self nor in the object without, but above all in the written discourse that is his 'measure'" (48).

We have noted the way in which Illich participates in this productive system of intertextuality. But his response to economic growth, to monetary proliferation, constitutes an objection not based upon an historical analysis but upon the same immediate denial with which he confronts the proliferation of textuality. In *Shadow Work*, a book that appeared a year before *Gender*, Illich writes: "Traditional cultures subsisted on sunshine . . . in these essentially sun-powered cultures, there was no need for language production" (66). Just as he must restrain the proliferation and displacement of meaning involved in intertextuality, so too he wants to restrain the proliferation of money. "Subsistence that is based on a progressive unplugging from the cash nexus," he tells us, "now appears to be a condition for survival" (Gender 17). "Whose survival?" we might ask.

The survival of women is supposed to be at stake—women are the losers. Yet his book gives testimony to the proliferation of women's writing, to their productivity, their displacements of meaning. One senses that it is primarily the rise of women's power, their increasing ability to shape and define meaning through discourse, that threatens Illich. They have moved into his territory. In this respect, it is telling that in the last chapters of *Gender* capitalism fails entirely as a mode of explanation. Instead, Illich turns to the church and its increasing associations with womanly functions.

If the language of transparency is associated with a valued past and a metaphorical power granted to the father, the language of the devalued present has taken on the metaphorical power of the mother. Illich details a transformation that echoes in interesting ways Ann Douglas's portrait of the feminization of American culture. Priests who formerly adhered to doctrine now become pastors devoted to care, nurturing, and the analysis of psyches. Illich calls this transformation the rise of the "monopoly of lactation" (160). The scorn he heaps on the church as "Alma Mater" parallels his jibes at the rise of the "taught mother tongue" that he claims replaces vernacular speech. Earlier, Illich seemed to valorize women's role as the source of life, but by the end of *Gender* it becomes clear that woman's motherly abilities and her metaphorical powers are finally objects of contempt.

In *Gender* then, the mother is both a powerful and threatening figure—not surprising in a book that looks for origins. But whereas feminists promote the power of the mother, Illich's fulmination against her at the end of his text reveals that he insists on a natural role for woman (a role that is opposed to a natural role for men) in order to keep woman in her place. His ways of describing the present are clearly misogynist; the present is not so much a unisex world as one in which women have circulated too far outside the home. The construction of difference, in other words, is for Illich a strategy of containment. Illich is threatened by the movement of women away from their "natural" place towards participation in the process of signification.

Of course, women, too, have assumed that language can be made to do what Illich tries to do, that is, represent authentic reality and essential differences. In the anthropological studies we have cited, the presentation of realities that are supposedly prior to language leads to surprising expressions of nostalgia. Nostalgia is understandable in a man threatened by the loss of his territory and prerogatives, but why are women writers attracted to the past and old territories of gender? As we have shown, a certain engagement with the past enhances authority: the past can function as a place where there was a stable referent, a decidable meaning. Women writers may share with men a nostalgia for this fictional locus of security. Furthermore, writers gain power by claiming to present "reality," since they seem then to be speaking *truth* itself. (To some extent, all of us embrace this aspiration to reveal the truth that is part of the writing process itself.) And there is another serious consideration for feminists: the positing of differences is necessary if the loss of difference is assumed to mean an *in*difference to women. We must carefully assess the political and ideological uses to which arguments that challenge the opposition *man/woman* can be put. But paradoxically, the insistence on difference can easily perpetuate sameness by setting up a fixed set of oppositions that produces stereotypes of men and women. At the end of his book, Illich writes that our hopes for the future depend on austerity, renunciation, and an "openness to surprise" (179). Yet by relying on stereotypes and a commitment to going backwards, surprise hardly seems possible. Not so if we think of identity and difference as constructed within language rather than preceding it. If differences are in the making, real surprise is possible. We look to the future.

Chapter
Six

Family
Feud

*I*n the past three decades, many writers have brandished their pens in the name of the family: not only scholars interested in the family as a sociological and historical phenomenon, but also more emotional polemicists on both the right and the left. None of these writers agree on what the family's place is in society, on the family's value, even on what we mean when we say "family." A representative example of this embattled writing is *The War Over the Family: Capturing the Middle Ground* by two well-known sociologists, Brigitte and Peter Berger. Entering into the heterogeneous discourse about the family, these two scholars—a family themselves (Brigitte claims the main argument and her husband the book's four excursi)—lead us to expect that their long-needed rational defense of the family will finally silence all debate. They are qualified authorities in the field and speak for, they believe, ordinary people like themselves who are, "tired of all the varieties of bullshit that have assailed us in recent years on the topic of the family" (Berger 52). What the

117

Bergers have to tell us is that in spite of all this hoopla, the family is not really a problem at all. They locate the "problem" elsewhere, in the "strident rhetoric" of those who have made the family a battle-ground. Unlike those noisy ideologues, the Bergers "believe that a rational and humane view of the family is essential for the future of mankind. We even believe (most audacious article of faith) that sociologists should write in English" (52). But the Bergers, so sensitive to the rhetoric of others, are not very sensitive to their own. Their polemical, supposedly unbiased text provides a telling example of a nostalgic story hostile to feminism.

The Bergers begin by describing the rhetorical positions of those who have turned the family into a "problem." There are three camps. The first includes leftists and feminists who see the family as a "nest of oppression and pathology" and as an obstacle to their liberation (17). The "pro-family" camp is primarily defined by its opposition to the first group. (Even though this camp's reactionary stance is formed in negative terms, it is "for the traditional family" [31].) The last is the "professional camp" that includes people of a "liberal-left bent" interested in defining the family as a problem so that their "helping" services appear necessary (35). The Bergers will try to negotiate a middle ground by clarifying the positions of these camps and appealing to a reality—the history of the family—against which conflicting claims about the family can be tested.

To this end, *The War Over the Family* is divided into three sections that are punctuated by several excursi: the first section analyzes the rhetoric about the family; the second section describes the history of the family; and the third, entitled "The Family—A Reasonable Defense," provides prescriptions for policy. This sequence suggests that the Bergers are holding back their own opinion until the end of the book. Indeed, the Bergers explicitly claim to be doing so, encouraging us to believe that their opinions are the product of objective analysis and historical truth, anything but the strident rhetoric proffered by other commentators on the family. Their book is what Peter Steinfels calls a "crusade against cant" (75).

In his book, *The Neo-Conservatives*, Steinfels argues that this crusade characterizes the neoconservative writing style. Though he does not discuss the Bergers, his scrutiny of other neoconservative texts helps delineate the strategies which lend the neoconservative style its credibility. That the Bergers rely on these strategies is not surprising; the Bergers' book comes out of their association with the "Mediating Structures Project" of the American Enterprise Institute, a conservative think-tank. Steinfels points out that neoconservatives attempt to stand at a distance from matters of conflict, a distance which apparently allows them to discover that many conflicts are irrelevant. Another neoconservative strategy is to provide grandiose solutions to problems. Steinfels says that these strategies "may diminish the issue, as typically occurred in neoconservatism's 'cooling' phase, when it argued that public 'crises' were largely the fantasies of crisis-mongering intellectuals; or the new definition may enlarge the issue, stretching it to the dimensions of civilization itself" (72). So, for example, in *The War Over the Family*, the Bergers stand back from the fray and provide a theoretical overview of the family, contemporary alignments, the discipline of sociology, which enables them to discover that the conflict over the family is surprisingly irrelevant to the family. This discovery allows them to dismiss the liberals' demand for government action ". . . on a wide array of issues supposedly relevant to the family, from such obvious ones as child care and women's rights to more-elusive [sic] ones (elusive, that is, in their bearing on family policy) such as 'comparable worth' of female occupations and even issues such as the environment, employment, and disarmament" (Berger 199). The Bergers then shift from supposedly irrelevant contemporary discussions about the family to consider the broad issue of the place of the family in history. Steinfels also notices the fondness of neoconservatives for displays of erudition. Neoconservatism, he says, ". . . is learned and sophisticated, with a wide range of references at its disposal. . ." (72). Like the authors Steinfels discusses, the Bergers establish our belief in their claims about the family through a learned vocabulary and a wide-range of scholarly references. Yet these features of academic discourse accompany an intention to speak for the common man in a language he can understand; the Bergers write to "give heart" to concerned individuals, to speak with humility for "ordinary" people. All these gestures distinguish neoconservative writers who present themselves as "the very sword and buckler of judiciousness, of good sense against nonsense" (Steinfels 75). It is with these weapons, with the aggression of an apparent reasonableness, that the Bergers will "capture" the middle ground, defending the "common sense of ordinary people" (ix).

What bothers Steinfels about strategies of the neoconservative style is that they allow a writer to "proclaim a high standard of discourse" and "uphold the values of 'rationality, moderation, balance and tolerance'" while the writer is actually too partisan to admit the complexity of an opponent's arguments or the elitism and ideological bias of his or her own position. As a result, says Steinfels, "neo-conservatives threaten to discredit the very values they aspire to serve" (79). Our analysis will demonstrate how useful neoconservative strategies are to the Bergers, but our point is a different one. We don't want to blame them for failing to live up to their own high standards. Instead, we want to show how the Bergers use an appeal to high standards to mask a militant, almost hysterical desire to contain women's identity, to keep the boundaries between masculine and feminine separate.

Feminists, because they represent a challenge to the nuclear family as natural, become an object of derision and fear for the Bergers. This derision is at least ironic, since the Bergers display an understanding of the social construction of reality (the title of one of Peter Berger's earlier books) and articulate misgivings about those who declare anything to be "natural." When describing class language, for example, they point out that "there is nothing 'natural' to these linguistic features [of class language]; rather, they are the result of social constructions which, in principle, could have come out very differently" (42). Yet despite their attentiveness to the social construction of reality, they still want an objective given, a stable referent without which they believe our very survival is at stake. What constitutes this given is the solid bedrock of the age-old family. "It is always foolish to gamble that all or even most of human experience up to one's instant in history has been a gigantic mistake. It is reckless to gamble with the moral heritage of an entire civilization" (Berger 193). This assertive defense of the family is clearly an emotional appeal, an appeal designed to gain our acceptance of a reality beyond rhetoric.

The Bergers negotiate the tension between their view of language and their need for reality with help from the work of the German sociologist Arnold Gehlen. Peter Berger introduced Gehlen's book *Man in the Age of Technology* to English-speaking readers and relies upon it in *The War Over the Family* to explain our instinctual need for an objective given. Gehlen nostalgically juxtaposes archaic institutions of a primitive society to modern institutions; as Peter Berger says in his introduction to Gehlen's book, "Archaic institutions are broadly encompassing and highly stable, thus approximating the functions of biological instincts; consequently, they provide very strong relief . . . Modernity 'deinstitutionalizes' in that it undermines the stability of institutions . . ." (Technology x). In *The War Over the Family*, the Bergers approvingly quote Gehlen on modern life: "The penetration of the experimental spirit into the arts and sciences of every kind has as a necessary consequence their objects' *loss of naturalness* [Bergers' emphasis]" (119). Or, as they put it, the "immediacy . . . of individual experience" gives way to "hyper-rationalization" (119). For the Bergers, the family is an archaic institution that allows for the kind of immediacy promised by Gehlen's primitive forms; feminism is an example of a "theme" of modernity that separates human beings from naturalness.

Peter Berger's explicit discussion of language in the first of his excursi, "Goshtalk, Femspeak, and The Battle of Language," can demonstrate how the construction of the natural is used as a political weapon against feminism. Here feminists are presented as mirror opposites of the Moral Majority; neither group is capable of understanding that "obscenity is a relative and socially constructed category" (42). In other words, Berger critiques bowdlerism from the point of view that nothing is inherently proper or improper in any use of language. He also aims to show how language, as a social construct, can be used as a political weapon. Both the Moral Majority and (more emphatically) feminists deny the political nature of "linguistic campaigns." Of feminists, Berger writes:

> In their mind, of course, there is no such thing [as "feminist language"]; there is only the correction of the "sexist" language used by others; it is *the others'* language that is political language (and the alleged politics of sexism are dissected in endless analytic exercises by feminist authors); *their own* language, preferably called "inclusive language" is supposedly nothing but the cleansing of speech from the nefarious political manipulations of the sexist oppressor (47).

Berger calls these unreflective feminists, "Femspeakers" (46).

But isn't Berger himself conducting a political campaign? Although he may think he stands above the fray in order to comment upon it, his arsenal of weapons includes examples that deflate and trivialize feminism and women writers who feel demeaned by certain uses of language—their feelings are those of "some little girl, say, who thought that she was not invited to a party because the masculine pronoun was used in the language of the invitation" (47)—and his reliance on a series of hostile and patronizing metaphors to characterize feminists. (Feminists at faculty meetings are alluded to as Salvation Army types [Berger 47].) Feminist concern about language is "a theory that elevates infantile misunderstandings to the level of hermeneutics" (48). Feminists attempt to "rewrite the classics in their deplorable idiom" just as a group of "demented clerics" are "translating the Bible . . . into the language of *Ms.* magazine" (50).

Feminists, in short, are grim moralists not given to humility and moderation. More than that, however, their concerns about language are "deafeningly trivial" because language is, Berger assures us, not really sexist (48). When he claims that sexism is the invention of feminists, he implies that we previously had an apolitical, proper language now being disturbed, or at least diminished, by their efforts. In other words, there *is* a natural language. He makes this point explicitly in his discussion of fascism: before Mussolini's castigation of the use of the pronoun *lei*, it had been "an apolitical and unreflective element of the common language" (Berger 49). Mussolini, says Berger, made what was "natural" into a political symbol, a process that presumably corresponds to the feminists' castigation of the apolitical use of the masculine pronoun as a generic term. For Berger, then, "it is *the others'* language that is political language" (47). Surely the blindness he has found in feminists, is, in fact, his own.

To impose order upon the chaos of rhetoric the Bergers see surrounding the topic of the family, they attempt to set up three distinct camps or "alignments." Yet, as the excursus on feminist language demonstrates, Peter Berger is unable to keep the practices of these groups separate from his own practices. He writes in the manner of those he condemns for using language as a weapon, even imitating their use of certain words (for example, "no bullshit"—his description of his own language—inadvertently aligns him with the new class who "talk dirty" but which he is condemning for other reasons.) Berger tells us that the basic purpose of all ideologically charged language is to draw boundaries; he then proceeds zealously to draw boundaries. But the inadequacy of these boundaries is revealed by his own inability to maintain them. Both his effort to impose boundaries—and his failure to maintain them—help us to recognize that he is partisan. He and Brigitte are hardly saving their opinion and defense "for later": in their supposedly objective overview of various rhetorical camps, they are already insisting upon the correctness of their opinion. And their opinion is that feminists are egregiously disrupting the natural, proper state of things.

The next step in the Bergers' analysis is to present new historical research supporting the hypothesis that "the nuclear family is a *pre-*

condition, rather than a *consequence*, of modernization" (87). The re-
visionist history they rely upon is derived from Peter Laslett's view
of the nuclear family as stable since the 16th century.[1] From this "history," they deduce that the nuclear family has not been produced by
industrialization and modernization, but instead is itself the origin of
change. As the Bergers say somewhat smugly, ". . . we believe that
the family has been a 'motor' of modernization in a way still not
perceived by most historians and social scientists. The latter continue
to perceive the family as, in the main, responding to changes outside
itself, to see it as a passive object of history, rather than as an active
agent" (105).

Though they claim this insight is a product of new historical research (as if there were now a consensus about the origin and development of the family), anyone who has read recent work on the
family knows that this "discovery" is neither the only nor the most
current view. The Bergers here simply echo the words of an article
on the family written in 1977, an article that itself refers to earlier
research. That article, "Family Time and Historical Time" by Tamara
K. Hareven, observes: "Particularly important has been a revision of
the traditional notion that the family broke down under the impact
of industrialization and urbanization. Rather than continuing to view
the family as a passive agent historical studies have revealed that the
role of the family was in fact that of an active agent" (58). Other,
contradictory views on the family proliferate. As Michèle Barrett and
Mary McIntosh point out in their excellent review of contemporary
social analyses of the family, this view runs counter to those of historians such as Michael Anderson who writes in his introduction to
Approaches to the History of the Western Family 1500–1914, "The West
has always been characterized by diversity of family forms, by diversity of family functions, and by diversity in attitudes to family
relationships not only over time but at any one point in time" (81).
Surely the Bergers are aware of recent historical accounts that con-
tradict their own—but they have chosen to supress them. The historian Mark Poster points out the ideological bias at the basis of historical accounts of the family which suppress diversity and conflict:
insistence on the sameness and continuity of the family renders the
family immutable, making it impossible to imagine alternatives past,
present, or future" (xix).[2]

The Bergers' narration of the history of the family not only renders
the family immutable but also constitutes it in the form of the individual it is supposed to produce. Speaking of the rise of the bourgeois

family, the Bergers write: "Only 'strong families' could shape 'strong characters,' and this the bourgeois family set itself to do— with, one must say, remarkable success" (111). As we have seen, and as the quotation demonstrates again, the family is an "active agent" that busily fosters change, produces individuals, nurtures them and their characters. In constructing the family as an "agent," the Bergers borrow from notions of subjectivity ideas that lend the family a coherent identity. Like the individual it produces, the family is autonomous, resilient, stable, and the locus of values. These characteristics make it an origin *outside of history*, a stable referent against which the Bergers can pose and evaluate spurious rhetorics. The value of the family is that it is a locus of rationality and individuality; those who repudiate it are selfish, irresponsible, authoritarian, "other" rather than "inner-directed" (Berger 171). (For evidence, the Bergers refer the reader to a number of texts, including Lasch's work on contemporary narcissism.) The family, then, is a coherent subject that produces a particular kind of consciousness, equally coherent and balanced.

The Bergers show no awareness of contemporary theoretical work that deconstructs the notion of this universalized, autonomous individual. These analyses demonstrate how oppositions are used to produce a truth that remains blind to the strategies of its own construction. We have already demonstrated a number of such oppositions: rhetoric/reality, ideological/apolitical, the values of balance and rationality juxtaposed with their opposites. But the major opposition the Bergers require in order to maintain the unity of the family and the individual is the opposition *male/female*. Though the Bergers describe the nuclear family as a "fine balance of revolutionizing activity in the larger society (the public sphere) and a zone of domesticity (the private sphere) . . .", many feminist critics have already shown that this "balance" relies upon the sexual division of labor (99). The Bergers never explicitly discuss this analysis because to do so would threaten their easy valorization of the family as a middle ground. This division, however, is everywhere implicit in their description of the family and the individuals it produces.

If we return to the first excursus for a moment, we can show how Peter Berger's dismissal of feminist scholarship in no way eliminates the problems that scholarship has exposed. Though the whole excursus works to encourage the reader to dismiss feminist concerns about language, this dismissal has its cost. Berger mocks feminists for criticizing the use of the masculine pronoun as a generic term (remember the little girls who misread their party invitations) but precisely because he insists upon using the masculine pronoun as a generic, he demonstrates more forcefully than he means to that the "strong" individual produced by the family is male. This problem is reflected in the text as a whole. For example, the Bergers write, "If it is the individual who is ultimately responsible for his [sic] actions, over against any group to which he [sic] belongs, then it is of the utmost importance to raise children in such a way that they will become 'men of conscience'" or "When the individual is responsible for himself [sic] and his [sic] career in this world, he [sic] becomes the center of life . . ." (110). And by refusing to talk about gender roles (because this is to speak in discredited feminist rhetoric), they dismiss, or relegate to a non-familial concern, a whole range of problems (abortion, gender roles, homosexuality, welfare) that feminists have analyzed and that can easily be identified in the text as products of, or challenges to, the nuclear family structure. Such inattentiveness to significant issues makes it quite unlikely that the Bergers can successfully umpire or resolve the debate over the family.

How are the oppositions that structure the "balance" of the family—public/private, active/passive, mind/body—part of a larger sexual opposition? After the Bergers enumerate all the values the family supposedly engenders, it becomes evident that the woman is the source, the ground, which produces them. So much so that the Bergers increasingly come to speak of the family as a *matrix*: "The bourgeois family has been the matrix (a singularly apt word in this context!) of a variety of values, norms, and 'definitions of reality'" (106). Matrix is indeed an apt word. The Bergers tell us that the "the woman is paramount in the home" where she is "seen as equal if not dominant" (101–2). Aware of the feminist critique of housework, the Bergers dismiss the notion that "only paid work is to be considered as supplying status" (101) and further argue that technology has greatly reduced housework anyway.[3] As the Bergers see it, woman's work in the home is rather elevated and abstract; hers is a "civilizing mission" (102). (This work, they tell us, is too hard for tired-out feminists: "Civilization-building is a weary-making task, with its own psychic costs" [103].)

It becomes increasingly clear that this glorified mission is primarily conducted through the reproductive and nurturing capacities of the mother. In the bourgeoisie "the family was sharply segregated from work . . . the household became a segregated locale for child-rearing. It was in this setting that the formation of 'strong characters,' of autonomous individuals imbued with an ethic of responsibility, could take place" (Berger 112). In her task as child-rearer, the mother is irreplaceable—neither the father nor outside agencies can perform this role (ironically, the Bergers learn this from the outside experts they so deplore). As the Bergers put it, the "minimal imperative" is a "stable" structure for the infant that is "tied to the mother" (152). They acknowledge a "theoretical possibility" that a male could be a "mother figure"—"though this is not too likely and for a simple reason: If such an arrangement were viable for the development of healthy infants, the vast variety of family arrangements in differing cultures would make one expect that it would have been successfully tried somewhere!" (Berger 152–53). This passage informs us that the mother's place is the stable referent that makes both the "unity" of the family and the individual himself possible. She creates a "'haven' of stable identity and meaning." Then, quoting an article written by Peter Berger and Hansfried Kellnor, "Marriage and the Construction of Reality," the Bergers remind us that this haven is a "world in which . . . he [sic] is somebody" (Berger 166).

Of course, it is when the woman demands that she too be somebody that the haven becomes destabilized, for it is at the expense of her individuality and energy that these possibilities are constructed. No wonder, then, that the Bergers' ire is directed against feminist demands for autonomy and career. The Bergers tell us, for example, that there is reason to agree with the pro-family camp's perception that feminists are hostile to children, willing to "dump children so that mothers can pursue their selfish programs of self-realization" (27). Feminists are hyper-individualists who make "brutal assertions of self against the claims of others (such as: notably children and spouses)" (120). There is not much discussion of child care in the Bergers' book except when it is casually thrown in a negative light, or when the authors are insisting that there be no government subsidy for it. In brief, the Bergers way of describing woman's proper role denies her individuality. For them, it is the male individual who is the active agent while the woman is the Rock of Gibraltar. She serves a passive and conservative function by providing a haven of stability, a timeless retreat where one's instinctual batteries can be recharged.

Mark Poster agrees with the Bergers that the family produces the "autonomous individual," but the difference in his rhetoric is telling. What Poster says is that

the bourgeois family structure is suited preeminently to generate people with ego structures that foster the *illusion* [our emphasis] that they are autonomous beings. Having internalized love-authority patterns to an unprecedented degree by anchoring displaced body energy in a super-ego, the bourgeois sees himself as his own self creation, as the captain of his soul, when in fact, he is the result of complex psycho-social processes (xix).

What Poster means by "love-authority patterns" is that, as the Bergers insist, the child in the bourgeois family is indeed the recipient of lots of love, *but* that there is a psychic cost:

The bourgeois family should be understood not simply as a progressive, morally beneficial nest of love, domesticity, the "wish to be free" and individualism, but as constituting a particular emotional pattern which served to . . . register in a unique way the conflicts of age and sex. In the bourgeois family, new forms of the oppression of children and women arose which were dependent upon critical mechanisms of authority and love, of intense ambivalent emotions (177).

Drawing upon Freud, Poster explains in more detail the "systematic exchange on the child's part of bodily gratification for parental love, which, in turn produces a deep internalization of the parent of the same sex. Sexual differences become sharp personality differences. Masculinity is defined as the capacity to sublimate, to be aggressive, rational and active; femininity is defined as the capacity to express emotions, to be weak, irrational and passive" (177). For these reasons, Poster argues that "the bourgeois family cannot survive a threat to sex-role differentiation" (199). If this is so, then the feminist demand for the individuality and autonomy of women not only challenges the family but also its way of structuring subjectivity. We are nothing so simple as "captains of our soul"—and the Bergers know this.

Though the Bergers want to reassure us that the nuclear bourgeois family is here to stay, their narration of the family's history is informed by a sense that it is already lost. In its most perfect incarnation, we are told, the family produced and maintained individuals who were balanced "between individualism and social responsibility, between 'liberation' and strong communal ties, between acquisitiveness and altruism" (117). This fine and "precarious" balance is now lost: "With this loss of balance, the enormous civilization-building power of the bourgeoisie is undermined and threatened, and the very notion of a bourgeois society is put in question" (117). To describe the result of this loss, the Bergers introduce a whole set of neologisms, " 'hyper-modernity' (with the subcategories of 'hyper-rationality' and 'hyper-individualism')" (118). This transformation hostile to the family was brought about by internal changes: the family contained "kernels of its disintegration" (118). The woman functions as this kernel; she is the center who kept the family in fine balance and now is its greatest threat, but the excesses of modernity have infected the woman and thrown the family off balance. Describing hyper-individuality, the Bergers say:

> The recent rise of feminism is important in this connection. The individual woman is now emphasized over against every communal context in which she may find herself—a redefinition of her situation that breaks not only the community between the spouses but (more fundamentally) the mother-child dyad, which, if anthropologists are correct, is the most basic human community of all (120).

The Bergers can only define community as the couple and the mother-child dyad. This inability to engage more complex definitions of community is both a cause of the claustrophobic feeling engendered by reading their book and a sign of their preoccupation with women's role in the home.

Despite their protestations to the contrary, the Bergers are clearly nostalgic for the "balance" of the nineteenth-century family, a balance crucially dependent upon the woman staying at home. Nostalgia, as we have demonstrated in preceding chapters, depends upon the juxtaposition of an idealized past to a decadent present, and it is in the excursus entitled "Are We Decadent?" that their nostalgia emerges most clearly. Here Peter Berger tells us that decadence *is* a conservative and nostalgic notion, but that "still, with proper care, the concept [of decadence] does have a certain usefulness" (131). "Taking proper care" means to him that we must avoid describing decadence in "organic" metaphors that might attach decadence to a notion of the natural. Instead of speaking in terms of the natural, he would rather speak in terms of an "objective given" so archaic that it appears inevitable. This objective given may not be natural, but it nonetheless grounds discourse in the same seemingly inevitable way by acting as a stable referent that we can all take for granted without thinking about it too much (a matter of common sense)—or, we can share in a common mourning for its loss. Peter Berger argues that we have lost something, a sense of this stable referent: "Decadence is a situation in which the central symbols of an institution, or of society as a whole, have become 'empty' or 'hollow'—that is, have lost an earlier power of providing meaning and identity" (131). More specifically, what happens in this situation is that "the family ceases to become an objective given . . . Everything—including, finally, 'gender roles,' sexuality, and child rearing—is uncertain, open to revision . . ." (132).

This nostalgic narrative of the loss of a referent, then, is a narrative of the loss of the mother as stable center at home. The Bergers' need for this referent is so strong that it shatters their veneer of intellectual respectability. We have seen how they have a self-consciousness about bad analysis, a self-consciousness that has no influence on their own practice. They dislike organic metaphors, but they use them: institutions contain the "kernel" of their own disintegration, the family is a "matrix that gives birth," and they rely upon a language of instinctual needs borrowed from Gehlen. They apparently detest neologisms while inventing terms like "femspeak," and even worse, "hyper-modernization," which apparently explains "counter-modernization." Finally, in the face of all their talk about loss, they claim they are not nostalgic. According to the Bergers, it is the talk about extended families that is nostalgic, though this, they insist, is a nostalgia for something that didn't exist. How could it exist when there has always been the nuclear family? The Bergers thus adhere to a belief in the immutability of the nuclear family: there have never been any alternatives to it in the past and there are no viable alternatives to it now (and so none for it in the future). It is surprising, then, that in his excursus on decadence, Peter Berger contradicts himself to say, "we are *not* conservatives in the sense of believing that this particular, historically relative family type is the only 'natural,' God-given, or immutable one" (133). Though in their book the Bergers attempt to draw a fine distinction between "God-given" and "objective-given" (a stable referent validated by time), these terms boil down to the same thing: the articulation of the family in terms which insist that it can not and will not change.

The contradiction that the Bergers never fully acknowledge is that if there are no viable alternatives to the bourgeois family, and if "ordinary" people understand this, then they don't need to write their defensive book. So why do they write? Their self-proclaimed defense is necessitated by their sense of loss—the loss of the patriarchal family of the nineteenth century, a loss for which feminists get the blame. As the book progresses, the portrayal of "feminists" becomes increasingly confused as the Bergers' response to the displacement of the father becomes more hysterical. Early in the book feminists are labelled as "anti-family." They are said to have a "missionary bent" (25), and, as we have seen, characterized as moralists of the Salvation Army type. This characterization aligns feminists with nineteenth-century "clerical-feminized" reformers (another simplification since all such reformers were not necessarily feminists). Feminists, say the Bergers, emphasize "self-realization," a quest which links them to the "California syndrome" (26–27). And feminism encourages "a widespread sense of the *relativity* of conventional family life. It greatly helped to give respectability to the notion of 'alternative lifestyles,' which made traditional sexual and family norms appear as just *one of many* ways of organizing these human concerns" (their emphasis) (26). Finally, feminists are described as anti-paternal. In sum, if feminists are moral, they are grimly so. If they want to be strong individuals, they are selfish. If they insist on the social construction of reality, they are fanatics (". . . the ERA movement provides the clearest expression of . . . a strongly, often fanatically anti-biological vision . . ." [57]). And if they challenge the authority of the father, they would "reduce" men "to docile drones in the new matriarchy" (189). Feminists cannot do anything with moderation, or the Bergers' rhetoric cannot let them do so.

The desire to represent the "middle ground" requires the Bergers to create extremes between which they can position themselves. So feminism must be created as an extreme term. The Bergers' narrative is fueled by their desire to maintain the woman, *particularly the woman as mother with child,* as a stable referent, a referent that helps maintain patriarchal power—and that feminists threaten. The animosity towards feminism that results from this emphasis on the referent encourages extreme representations. The stable referent itself, the mother-child dyad, is articulated in equally extreme terms to emphasize its importance as "the most basic human community of all" (120). But the Bergers' reliance on extremes and oppositions to structure their argument causes an unexpected problem: In the last Excursus, "Father-Mother-Child," Peter Berger finds himself in league with the feminists he most despises. His own extremity has caught up with him.

The excursus begins with a consideration of whether the mother-child dyad is a natural or universal symbol. We are back to the question of the referent again. Peter Berger both wants, and doesn't want, the mother to play the role of the referent—as his effort to delineate three types of feminism makes clear. The first, an increasingly conservative type of feminism, would emphasize the mother's biological, nurturing role.[4] The second, promoted by feminist spiritualists, valorizes a Mother-Goddess who is also posited as a natural origin. The third, directly opposed to the essentialism of these two, continues to call into question the mother's traditional role and to emphasize the power relations that constitute the family. Since all of these feminisms have in common the displacement of the father's privileges and power, Berger denigrates them. But in deploring those who exalt the mother-child dyad, he confuses the reader: up to this point he has fully endorsed this dyad's importance. What Berger ends up saying is, in effect, that the feature of the family that preserved its balance now threatens to destabilize it. "Father-mother-child. We know the wealth of human values that this litany alludes to. Could a similar wealth be hidden in the dyadic formula of mother-child? We doubt it very much indeed . . . we know too much about children to be sanguine about the degradation of fatherhood" (192–93). Throughout the text the Bergers have downplayed the importance of the father and valorized the mother, suppressing the way the father's power and authority are maintained by the woman's role in the home. Now Berger wants to reassert the father. But on what grounds? After lamely toying with "nature" and "God" as sanctions for his place, Berger resorts to reciting a nursery rhyme (he only remembers the beginning) that goes "Father-Mother-Child" and insisting upon the primacy of the father and the danger of his "degradation."

"Father-Mother-Child," the mother is restored as the middle term. Public-family-private, so is the family. This middle ground, apparently a locus of balance, is a site of conflict, a "kernel" of disintegration. The Bergers' text, which itself poses as a middle ground, is another site of division rather than balance. Though *The War Over the Family* is coauthored, a product of literal as well as authorial marriage, husband and wife are relegated to separate spheres. In the preface, they write:

The nature of our collaboration should be specified. This book is, in the main, Brigitte Berger's. It was her idea, the design and the central argument of the book are hers, and family sociology has been one of her areas of specialization for many years. Peter Berger has contributed various theoretical perspectives, especially in the area of modernization. He is also responsible for the four excursi in the book. The basic approach, both intellectually and in terms of partisanship, is common to both authors (viii).

At first glance, this division of labor seems, if anything, to privilege Brigitte. She, the mother of the book, is especially interested in the family ("the central argument" is hers). Yet not only her topic but also her labor—traditional research and summary—contrast in familiar ways with Peter's theoretical perspective and polemical freedom. She is the base, the matrix perhaps, that provides the ground from which Berger ascends—his excursi provide a lofty meditation on the concerns of the text. Within the mediating structure of coauthorship, then, a hierarchical division remains in place.

On the level of style there are even more dramatic reminders that the much-vaunted middle ground is an absent ideal. Although the authors claim to be modest and rational, they create extremes and confuse distinctions that would maintain them as the middle ground. Further, they never arrive at the promised end, the moment when they will "capture" that elusive middle ground. The reader's expectations of this moment are continually deferred as the Bergers repeatedly cut short analysis: "we will hold back on our own view of these matters, leaving that for later presentation" (53), "this is not the place to discuss" (63), "this cannot be the place to trace" (66), "a pursuit of these broad questions would exceed our present purpose" (89), "we cannot develop this point here" (123). And in place of the missing analysis, the Bergers substitute assertions that they repeat and repeat. Ironically, this practice becomes intolerable in the final section of the book, entitled "The Family—A Reasonable Defense." For too long, the Bergers have lead the reader to expect something that simply isn't there. In the end, they can only repeat what they have already said in an increasingly nasty and agitated way. The family is said to be in danger of degenerating into a "public convenience" (177), while the Bergers continue to assert that all is well with the family. Even in their resolution the family remains a site of conflicting interpretations, interpretations of their own making.

The language of the Berger's text, then, does not function to make the family a stable truth. And it is not just what they say, but how they say it that makes it so difficult to believe that their words are anchored to an "objective given," to common sense, to basic institutions and truths. Even at the level of the paragraph and sentence, the Bergers' rhetoric provides a vivid example of language adrift. Here is a passage representative in length and obscurity:

This is highly relevant to our understanding of the relation of the family to modern society. We must distinguish between modern institutions and modern consciousness. It is quite correct that modern institutions produce modern consciousness. Thus, as the family is subjected to such modern processes as urbanization and industrialization, family values, norms, and concepts undergo changes. This does not mean, as we have indicated before, that all premodern forms of ideation simply disappear; with whatever modifications, or even with very few modifications, these traditional structures of consciousness may survive long into the modern period. But what is more, we can find (both historically and today) that modern structures of consciousness antedate their 'realization' in modern institutions. Logically, of course, this had to be so in the beginning. Thus modern science and (at least by implication) modern technology had first to appear in the minds of innovative individuals before they began to be realized in the transformation of the external social world. But even today there can be a 'cultural lag' in the opposite way from the usual sociological understanding of this phrase—that is, modern institutions may 'lag behind' the appearance of certain elements of modern consciousness. A good example of this is the effect on consciousness of even a very minor injection of modern mass communication into a traditional situation, in consequence of which modern ideas began to circulate in this situation *prior* to any concrete institutional change. In just this way, the new historical research on the family suggests that the Western nuclear family, long before the advent of modernization, fostered mind-sets and values that were instrumental in bringing about institutional modernization, perhaps even in a very decisive way (90–91).

What are they saying here? One translation might be: "modern institutions have an effect on the family and shape consciousness, though these institutions are themselves a product of earlier forms of consciousness, fostered in part by the family." The Bergers are offering, then, a sort of chicken-and-egg argument that predictably asserts the primacy of the individual and the family. And what are we to make of the style of this passage? With characteristic imprecision, the paragraph is full of demonstrative pronouns—"this is highly relevant," "this does not mean," "this had to be so"—lacking clear referents. Notice, too, that all these phrases are in the form of assertions. When logical connectives are used—"thus" appears twice—they are not earned but rather create the semblance of argument. And even these speciously conclusive sentences are followed by sentences that begin with "but," a mark of disjunction that signals a contradictory assertion. Read enough paragraphs like this and the reader is certain to believe that something is indeed lost—the referent so valued by those who claim to write plain English.

Representation itself is the major obstacle to the presentation of an objective given, as the clumsiness of the Bergers' prose makes obvious. Like each of the other authors we have discussed, the Bergers are yearning for something that never was. But not only does their rhetoric create the "balance" of the family of the past, it also insures that the meaning of the family will begin to slide. Feminists are blamed. They are blamed by the Bergers, and by some feminists too. Betty Friedan, Germaine Greer, Jean Elshtain, for example, have all expressed concern about feminism's effect on founding structures, life forces, and of course, the family as the home of all natural truths about men and women.[5] Yet, as we have shown, it is not some grim, extremist feminism but the *volubility* of both feminists and their detractors that is to blame. Discourse has taken possession of father-mother-child and made them into characters of a story told, retold, and revised, with ever-increasing frequency. By subverting the strong efforts of writers like the Bergers—and the other nostalgic writers we have examined—to hide the linguistic and ideological basis of the "truths" they wish to promulgate, feminist theory opens up the discourse about "founding structures" for analysis and for new, resisting voices.

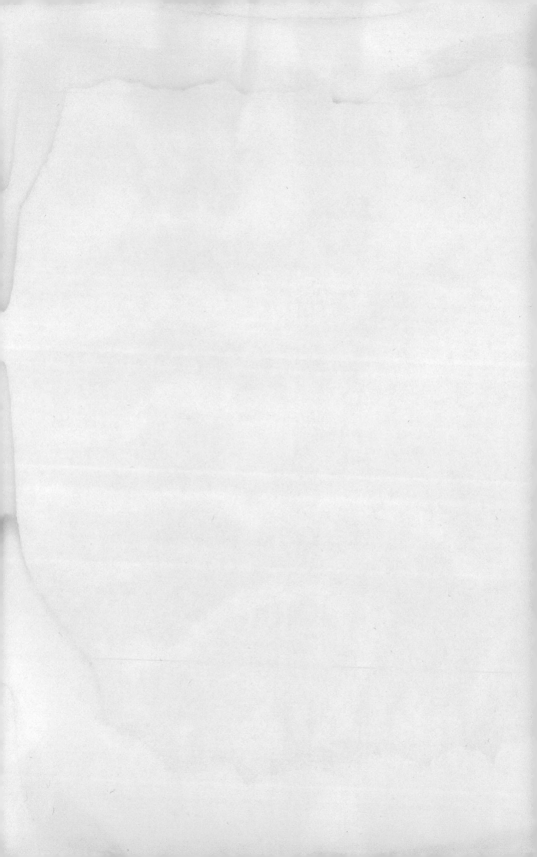

Postscript

ate Millett's *Sexual Politics*, written almost twenty years ago, remains a powerful analysis of a "counterrevolutionary" response to what she calls the "first phase" of the sexual revolution, the period between 1830 and 1930. Male "counterrevolutionaries" met the challenge of the women's movement, particularly its claim that the "distinctions between the sexes . . . have essentially cultural . . . bases," with an adamant assertion that distinctions between the sexes were biological (50). The objects of Millett's scrutiny, psychologists, sociologists, anthropologists and novelists writing between 1930 and 1960, bear an uncanny resemblance to the contemporary nostalgic writers that we have discussed. Describing a book that she calls a definitive "statement of counterrevolutionary attitude," Millett notes that it advertises "the Middle Ages as a golden period of sanity" (278) and advocates a "return to the old instinctive ways, never actually defined, yet always asserted to be better" (281). Is history repeating itself?

Millett did not predict such a repetition. In the closing remarks of her book, she writes that "there is evidence in the last few years that the reactionary sexual ethic . . . has nearly spent itself" (473). Our analysis of the nostalgic response to feminists like Millett herself suggests that we cannot now be so optimistic, though significant changes have occurred. For one thing, the nostalgia Millett so casually mentions as a feature of "counterrevolutionary" writing has become a more insistent national preoccupation, one significantly encouraged by the proliferation of feminist texts that Millett herself helped to stimulate. Nostalgic writers blame women for challenging the power of the paternal text to represent the real. The terms of the argument, then, have changed. *Textual* practices are in the foreground.

Another way in which our analysis diverges from Millett's is in our discussion of the writings of feminists themselves. In these writings the existence of sexual difference is now a matter of much debate. Some feminist writers are concerned to emphasize biological differences that they feel define feminine identity, particularly a woman's identity as a mother. Others see sexual difference as a cultural construction that preserves the possibility of salvaging a distinctly feminine identity and ethics. Yet other feminist writers are willing to risk the essentialism associated with the assertion of difference in order to insure that "woman" will not disappear into an undifferentiated male discourse. Those who "risk" essentialism are uneasy about privileging difference, but see it as a protest against male post-structuralist critics who wish to create a new stereotype of women: "woman" as a metaphor for representation. All of these writers, whether or not they perceive difference to be an "essential" reality, insist upon sexual difference in order to offer women a privileged position. As it does in the nostalgic system we analyze, difference valorizes one side of a polar opposition.

The seductive appeal of the feminist assertion of difference depends on its use of a structure of opposition. The assertion of difference gives women something tangible to affirm, a stable referent instead of the vertigo that comes when identity, so long linked to sexual difference, begins to slip. It could, of course, be argued that effective political action depends on women's ability to define themselves as different, as a distinct group. Yet even that so sensible perception underestimates the connection between the decentralization of the feminist movement and its strength: because there are many feminisms, the movement does not depend on the fortunes of a single leader or group. We are accustomed to think in terms of the powers associated with accumulation and identity rather than of the powers associated with dispersion and rupture precisely because the conventions of discourse, based on binary oppositions that preserve identity, insist that we do. "Woman" is not likely to disappear right away.

We have talked about how the nostalgic writer blames feminists for the loss of paternal authority, of the referent itself. Nostalgic writers assert difference, especially sexual difference, to stave off a growing sense of the decentering powers of language so frequently associated with the feminine. Should feminists be happy to find themselves so positioned, tied to modernity and an unstable discourse? What our work has shown is that this question is less esoterically theoretical than it is sometimes made out to be. Certainly French feminist theorists have insisted on the conjunction between femininity and the disruption of stable referentiality, but the writers we have analyzed do much the same thing—and they do not read French feminist writings. This conjunction suggests that problems of language and "woman" have now invaded all kinds of writing: ours is, whether we will or no, a moment of epistemological crisis that is insistently imagined in gendered terms.

While French feminists celebrate this crisis, nostalgic writers, finding themselves subject to the powers of language to disrupt their desire for mastery, integrity, and truth, become melancholy. We are more sanguine. Our analysis has shown that the desire to fix meaning has been used against women, particularly against their authority. We have seen, for example, how nostalgic writers try to contain in one image the diversity of resistance to oppression that the feminist movement has offered. This representative feminist is a monstrous Amazon whose writing must be domesticated to protect paternal authority. Lasch, Irving, and Bloom write to defend culture from "feminization"—for them the loss of the "real"—and also from feminists who write too much and so challenge paternal authority, a patriarchal literary tradition, and the illusion of male autonomy and subjectivity. That autonomy is challenged, as our analysis of the work of Ivan Illich demonstrates, by the condition of intertextuality that confuses male and female spheres. The Bergers, suffering challenges to the patriarchal family in which the mother functions as a stable referent, are no more able than the others to find a secure place within discourse from which to anchor language, woman, and the father's authority. They cannot escape the conditions of discourse. Nor can we, nor do we

141

want to. Nostalgic writers resist feminism by fixing sexual difference, sometimes appropriating the work of feminists themselves. By embracing the subversive possibilities of language, feminist theorists can undermine nostalgic rhetoric, leaving cultural definitions of masculinity and femininity in play, rather than in place.

Notes

Introduction

[1] George Gilder writes in his acknowledgments, "I was introduced to the subject by feminists so appealing and persuasive that it took several enjoyable years to discover that they were wrong." He then gives thanks to specific feminist friends.

[2] This curious remark of Gilder's is to be found in his acknowledgments.

[3] The announcement that Gilder's book is about to be reissued in a new edition came in an editorial by William Buckley, Jr. (*The Washington Post*, February 19, 1986). Buckley begins by decrying the rise in illegitimate births to blacks and then turns to the social problems caused by the sexual revolution: "The objective shortage of young, unmarried women willing to marry young, unmarried men, so many of them electing, instead, to marry older, successful men, breeds not

children, but social problems" (A21). Like any number of other contemporary writers, Buckley wants to encourage young women to marry and have children as quickly as possible by damning their independence as a cause of American's problems.

[4] See Ti-Grace Atkinson's *Amazon Odyssey* (New York: Links Books, 1974).

[5] See Shulamith Firestone's *The Dialectic of Sex: The Case for Feminist Revolution* (New York: William Morrow, 1970).

[6] See Kate Millett's *Sexual Politics* (New York: Doubleday, 1970). We discuss *Sexual Politics* in more detail in the postscript.

[7] The writings of Jacques Derrida investigate this structure of opposition. See, for example, *Of Grammatology*, translated by Gayatri Chakravorty Spivak (Baltimore and London: The Johns Hopkins University Press, 1976), including her fine "Translator's Preface." For an example of a feminist analysis of systematic structures of opposition see Shoshana Felman, "Women and Madness: The Critical Phallacy," *Diacritics* (Winter, 1975), pp. 2–10.

[8] For an analysis of this kind of feminist writing, see Alice Echols, "The New Feminism of Ying and Yang," in *Powers of Desire*, ed. Ann Snitow, Christine Stansell, and Sharon Thompson (New York: Monthly Review Press, 1983, pp. 440–59).

[9] See, for example, Mary Daly, *Gyn/Ecology* (Boston: Beacon Press, 1978); Carol Gilligan, *In a Different Voice: Psychological Theory and Women's Development* (Cambridge, Mass.: Harvard University Press, 1982); and Germaine Greer, *Sex and Destiny* (New York: Harper and Row, 1984).

[10] As an example of this, we might cite an article in the neoconservative journal *Chronicles* (June, 1986), "Old Adam, New Eve," by Thomas Fleming. Fleming lambastes feminist fiction and scholarship, which apparently "plans to drag an entire society against the grain of human nature" (15). Yet he allows for the following exceptions: "Not all feminists or 'womens studies' scholars are liars or lesbians. A good many of them are making important contributions to their disciplines, precisely because they concentrate on the uniqueness of the feminine experience. A few names come immediately to mind: Alice S. Rossi for her studies of women students, Niles Newton for her exploration of the complex eroticism of the female sex, Ann Doug-

las for her observations on the feminization of 19th-century America, Carol Gilligan for her often dotty but sometimes sensible remarks on female ethics. . . . What all these writers share is the realization that boys and girls are different and an awareness of the significance of those differences" (9).

[11] In the same way, we must also qualify our relationship to those French feminists who offer a poststructuralist critique of phallocentric language. We are in sympathy with, and have learned much from, the deconstructive strategies of these writers. Yet we remain uneasy about their advocacy of an alternative discourse that appears to be linked to bodily difference and libidinal drives. For her sophisticated awareness of the operation of language, we do, however, recommend the reader to the recently translated work of Luce Irigaray. See her *Speculum of the Other Woman*, translated by Gillian C. Gill (Ithaca, New York: Cornell University Press, 1985) and *This Sex Which Is Not One*, translated by Catherine Porter with Carolyn Burke (Ithaca, New York: Cornell University Press, 1985). For a sampling of Irigaray and other French feminists, see *New French Feminisms*, ed. Elaine Marks and Isabelle de Courtivron (Amherst: University of Massachusetts Press, 1980).

1. *Monstrous Amazons*

[1] See Toril Moi's *Sexual/Textual Politics* (London and New York: Methuen, 1985) especially pages 42–49, for a cogent critique of a feminist literary criticism that borrows from humanism. Moi points out that the humanist notion of self as unitary, integrated, and autonomous is inevitably a "phallic self constructed on the model of the self-contained powerful phallus" (8). Moi's analysis gives support to our argument that by promoting the ideal of the humanist self, *Regiment of Women* attempts to ground itself upon the universal truth of the phallus.

[2] In his *New York Times* article, "Sexism, Racism and Black Women Writers," Watkins cites several examples of the negative portraits of black males in black women's writing, but adds that "These examples are not meant to suggest the majority of fiction by black women is focused on black male brutality. Recent novels, such as Alice Walker's *Meridian*, Ntozake Shange's *Betsey Brown*, Gloria Naylor's *Linden Hills*,

Ellease Southerland's *Let the Lion Eat Straw*, Rosa Guy's *Measure of Time* and nearly all of Toni Morrison's works generally, do not deal with the subject of black male oppression" (35). Watkins is trying to show that not all black women writers garner success by focusing their writing on the supposed brutality of black men. Our point is that it does not matter what women write about. We suspect that the very volume of writing by black women is perceived by some black male writers as a threat to their authority.

³ This is the "true story" that Ian Ball wants to write. Becky, however, insists upon reversing the plot; in the final version of Ball's play the black man is made responsible for the reckless eyeballing and the white woman is vindicated. The reader is not allowed to forget that Ian changes his play only because feminists pressure him into this plot reversal. Like *Regiment of Women*, *Reckless Eyeballing* envisions feminist demands as a simple cry for power reversal: women want to dominate men.

⁴ In an excellent article, "Melodramas of Beset Manhood: How Theories of American Fiction Exclude Women Authors," Nina Baym discusses the restrictive implications of these conventions for women writers, especially as these conventions have been formulated by male critics of American literature who decide what comprises literary excellence. Baym describes the central convention of American literature, the "myth of America," as ". . . a confrontation of the American individual, the pure American self—divorced from specific social circumstances, with the promise offered by the idea of America. . . . Behind this promise is the assurance that individuals come before society, that they exist in some meaningful sense prior to, and apart from, societies in which they happen to find themselves. The myth also holds that, as something artificial and secondary to human nature, society exerts an unmitigatedly destructive pressure on individuality" (71). A gender dichotomy is set up in these terms: women are "experienced as a source of social power" from which the male protagonist must escape, usually into the wilderness. Baym further points out that women's writing is also experienced as representing the wrongheaded "consensus" of society; American authors have thus long imagined themselves as pitted against the creators of the bad best-seller, typically women.

2. Feminism and the Decline of America

[1] Robert Westbrook, in "Good-bye to All That: Aileen Kraditor and Radical History," uses the term "radical traditionalist" to describe radical intellectuals who "share the neo-conservatives' concern with and for mediating institutions" and an "animus to centralized state power and to the 'new class' of professionals and managers" (85–86).

[2] Lasch offers a "realistic perception of decline" as one of three explanations for nostalgia, claiming that his explanation "has never gained much currency" because people do not like to hear bad news" (Politics 68). Lasch angrily defended himself against charges that he is nostalgic in a symposium on *Culture of Narcissism* published in *Salmagundi*, 46 (1979). That symposium included the first version of this chapter. In his response, Lasch suggested that we were "impermeable to rational argument," then went on to say "Doane and Hodges, like many other intellectuals, can't seem to see what is readily apparent to ordinary men and women" (199). We will discuss the appeal to "ordinary people" in Chapter Seven.

Charles Altieri, in an excellent article "Ecce Homo: Narcissism, Power, Pathos, and the Status of Autobiographical Representation," has used the Salmagundi symposium on *Culture of Narcissism* as a basis for considering the social critic's temptation to self-idealization and Nietzsche's ways of resisting fantasies of power.

[3] Fred Siegel, in "The Agony of Christopher Lasch," demonstrates the links between Lasch's recent essays and his earlier work: "Lasch's contentions about patriarchy, feminism, the cult of experience, and the dangers of social engineering which have made him the white crow of the American left were already fully developed in his first major work, *The New Radicalism in America*, although they were presented there without any of the Freudian trappings he has recently adopted" (285–86).

[4] For an exceptionally lucid introduction to Lacan's work, particularly as it engages the debate on feminine sexuality, see Jacqueline Rose's "Introduction—II" in *Feminine Sexuality: Jacques Lacan and the école freudienne*.

[5] Lois Chaber has published a fine defense of Moll Flanders, "Matriarchal Mirror: Women and Capital in *Moll Flanders*," that discusses

the "problematic 'crime' of prostitution" and the critical responses to it (214).

3. *Women and the Word According to* Garp

[1] Jenny's writing could thus be considered as Irving's implicit response to the feminist question: What if we replace the patriarch, the paternal premise of the novel, with the matriarch, or a maternal premise? His answer—a strong matriarch begets not a coherent, logically consecutive narrative sequence, but a more formless and disharmonious story—differs from similar claims about women's writing by some feminist literary critics only in that Irving's novel denigrates this sort of writing and valorizes narrative coherence (and thus coherent identity). Jenny's writing is not allowed to speak in *The World According to Garp*, with the exception, appropriately enough, of her one coherent *thesis* sentence. The interesting coincidence of Irving's assumptions about women's writing and those of some feminist literary critics—that women's writing is more formless, fluid, amorphous than men's writing—reminds us of how much such an assumption is ideologically based upon stereotypes of sexual identity rather than on women's "nature."

[2] Sandra Gilbert and Susan Gubar discuss this equation at length in *The Madwoman in the Attic: The Woman Writer and the Nineteenth Century Literary Imagination*, particularly pp. 3–16.

[3] Said and Brooks, in other words, may be responding, however indirectly, to the same fear as Irving's—the rise of women's authority. It seems more than coincidence that Edward Said's *Beginnings* and Peter Brooks's *Reading for the Plot* make their argument about narrative as essentially the *son's* story in both theme and structure at a time when women are making a case for the importance of women novelists. These two critics' neglect of women writers, however, does not necessarily invalidate their argument, which essentially suggests that the novel—a genre most obviously in the service of social and material reality—preserves patriarchal notions of identity and sexual difference.

Feminist critics, such as Susan Gubar and Sandra Gilbert, and more recently Dianne Sadoff, have amply demonstrated the anxieties of authorship that burdened those nineteenth-century women writers who confronted and took literally the powerful metaphorics of patriarchal authority. See *The Madwoman in the Attic* and Dianne F. Sadoff, *Monsters of Affection: Dickens, Eliot, and Brontë on Fatherhood*, particularly Chapters 2 and 3. Yet, as Nancy Armstrong has reminded us, women *did* write in the nineteenth century and the novel was perceived to be a remarkably congenial form: a notion of feminine authority was both *responsible for* and *enabled by* the rise of the novel as a literary genre. See her article, "The Rise of Feminine Authority in the Novel." As Armstrong points out, however, this feminine authority was still very much in the service of a patriarchal culture primarily because it was dependent upon the broader ideological split between distinct and separate spheres—the male public sphere and the female private and domestic sphere. The novel, which exalted "the private, the domestic and dealt with the affairs of the heart," seemed a "natural" outlet for feminine authority. While women's novels may seem to present stories of women's experience and feelings, as Armstrong shrewdly points out what we are getting instead is "not female nature or female culture, strictly speaking, but ideology and cultural myth" (138). She notes, however, that ". . . various attempts to define femininity in rigid opposition to masculinity necessarily fail . . . because sexuality proves to be nothing less than a language" (145).

Armstrong writes from a very different perspective than do Brooks and Said, and the two perspectives may seem at first glance contradictory. Is the novel's authority a patriarch who begets narrative sequence just as he does the family line? Or is the novel's authority feminine and domestic? Essentially both perspectives demonstrate the degree to which the traditional novel preserves patriarchal notions of identity and sexual difference. And we might point out that both perspectives are operating in *Garp*. Garp is, by the end of the novel, the father *par excellence*, but he is also "feminized" because he takes charge of the domestic sphere—staying home to raise the children, cook, and clean so that he can write while Helen goes off to the public sphere to earn money. (Did anyone else wonder how he found the time?) Garp's domesticity may look like a feminist reversal of roles; from Armstrong's perspective, it could also look like a male appropriation of a female sphere that "authorized feminine discourse" (Armstrong, 133).

4. *The Anxiety of Feminist Influence*

[1] Annette Kolodny's more sophisticated critique of Bloom differs from that of other feminists in that she does not posit an authentic self or female psychology as the basis for the alternative canon she would construct. She defines women readers and writers within a cultural network of meanings and symbols. See her "A Map for Misreading: or, Gender and the Interpretation of Literary Texts."

5. *Feminist Scholarship as Shadow Work*

[1] See also Elizabeth Janeway, as quoted in Chapter Three, pp. 67–68.

[2] In this article, Vance himself imagines a past in which language is clear and real because it is the product of a world that is seemingly without exchange.

[3] In *Shadow Work*, Illich refers to vernacular woman as *femina domestica* and vernacular man as *vir laborans*. He also labels the inhabitants of the present as "impotent." See *Shadow Work*, p. 113.

6. *Family Feud*

[1] See Peter Laslett, *The World We Have Lost* (New York: Scribner, 1965). See also Peter Laslett and Richard Walls, eds., *Household and Family in Past Time* (New York: Cambridge University Press, 1972).

[2] Nancy Theriot, in her monograph *Nostalgia on the Right*, offers a cogent summary of the nostalgia for the immutable family that never was: "White middle-class experience of dramatic social change triggered the idealization of family in the nineteenth century; today, white middle-class fear of uncontrollable social, economic, and cultural forces prompts a general nostalgia for a past that never was, a half-invented and half-hoped for memory of family tranquillity" (12).

[3] Many recent studies of housework argue that women today spend as much time on housework as they did in the past. What has changed is simply the kinds of tasks that constitute this work.

[4] Brigitte Berger's attachment to the idea of nurturing as the true role for women stands in tension with her professional role as a scholar and writer, a tension we can all understand. The very pressures of work make nostalgic fantasies of the home very seductive. As Nancy Theriot writes: "Family ideology offers women an escape from the choice and confusion of culture (the world) into the sureness and comfort of nature (home and family). The temptation of immanence, the invitation of the home, is difficult for modern women to resist because the world offers women what it offers men (only for less pay): alienated labor and disrupted community" (37).

[5] Judith Stacey argues that Friedan and Elshtain, in their recent work, "reflect and fuel broader antifeminist and politically reactionary development in their writings" (561). See Stacey's fine article on this subject, "The New Conservative Feminism," in *Feminist Studies*, 3 (Fall, 1983), pp. 559–83. Nancy Theriot challenges new groups on the left who wish to restore family strength saying "because the ideal [of the family] is rooted in commercial/industrial capitalism and is built on a 'naturalistic' view of sex roles, it has no place in a progressive proposal for social change" (37).

References

Altieri, Charles. "Ecce Homo: Narcissism, Power, Pathos, and the Status of Autobiographical Representation." *boundary 2* 9:3, (Spring-Fall, 1981): 389–413.

Anderson, Michael. Approaches to the History of the Western Family 1500–1914. As quoted in *The Anti-Social Family*, by Michèle Barrett and Mary McIntosh. London: Verso/NLB, 1982.

Armstrong, Nancy. "The Rise of Feminine Authority in the Novel." *Novel: A Forum on Fiction* 15 (Winter 1982): 127–45.

Atkinson, Ti-Grace. *Amazon Odyssey*. New York: Links Books, 1974.

Barthes, Roland. *The Pleasure of the Text*, trans. Richard Miller. New York: Hill and Wang, 1975.

Barthes, Roland. *S/Z*, trans. Richard Miller. New York: Hill and Wang, 1974.

Baym, Nina. "Melodramas of Beset Manhood: How Theories of American Fiction Exclude Women Authors." In *The New Feminist*

Criticism: Essays on Women, Literature and Theory, ed. Elaine Show-alter. New York: Pantheon Books, 1985, 63–80.

Benjamin, Walter. *Illuminations*, trans. Harry Zohn, ed. Hannah Arendt. New York: Harcourt, Brace and World, 1968.

Berger, Brigitte and Peter L. Berger. *The War Over the Family: Capturing the Middle Ground*. Garden City: Anchor Press/Doubleday, 1984.

Berger, Peter. Foreword to *Man in the Age of Technology*, by Arnold Gehlen. New York: Columbia University Press, 1980.

Berger, Thomas. *The Regiment of Women*. New York: Simon and Schuster, 1973.

Bloom, Harold. *The Anxiety of Influence: A Theory of Poetry*. New York: Oxford University Press, 1973.

Bloom, Harold. *A Man of Misreading*. New York: Oxford University Press, 1975.

Boserup, Esther. *Women's Role in Economic Development*. New York: St. Martin's Press, 1974.

Braudy, Leo. Review of *Regiment of Women* by Thomas Berger. *The New York Times*, 13 May 1973: 7:6.

Brooks, Peter. *Reading for the Plot: Design and Intention in Narrative*. New York: Alfred A. Knopf, 1984.

Chaber, Lois. "Matriarchal Mirror: Women and Capital in *Moll Flanders*." *PMLA* 97 (March 1982): 212–26.

Clecak, Peter. *America's Quest for the Ideal Self*. New York and London: Oxford University Press, 1983.

Daly, Mary. *Gyn/Ecology*. Boston: Beacon Press, 1978.

De Lauretis, Teresa. *Alice Doesn't: Feminism, Semiotics, Cinema*. Bloomington: Indiana University Press, 1984.

Derrida, Jacques. *Of Grammatology*, trans. Gayatri Chakravorty Spivak. Baltimore and London: The Johns Hopkins University Press, 1976.

Dickstein, Lore. Review of *Regiment of Women*, by Thomas Berger. *Ms.* November 1973: 32–34.

Douglas, Ann. *The Feminization of American Culture*. New York: Alfred A. Knopf, 1977.

Echols, Alice. "The New Feminism of Yin and Yang." In *Powers of Desire*, ed. Ann Snitow, Christine Stansell, and Sharon Thompson. New York: Monthly Review Press, 1983. 440–59.

Eisenstein, Hester. Introduction. *The Future of Difference*, eds. Hester Eisenstein and Alice Jardine. Boston: G.K. Hall & Co., 1980.

Engel, Stephanie. "Femininity as Tragedy: Re-examining the 'New

Narcissism'." *Socialist Review* 10:5 (September-October, 1980): 77–104.

Etienne, Mona and Eleanor Leacock, eds. *Women and Colonization: Anthropological Perspectives.* New York: Praeger, 1980.

Felman, Shoshana. "Women and Madness: The Critical Phallacy." *Diacritics* (Winter 1975): 2–10.

Firestone, Shulamith. *The Dialectic of Sex: The Case for Feminist Revolution.* New York: William Morrow, 1970.

Foucault, Michel. Afterword to *Michel Foucault: Beyond Structuralism and Hermeneutics,* Hubert L. Dreyfus and Paul Rabinow. 2nd ed. Chicago: The University of Chicago Press, 1983.

French, Marilyn. "The 'Garp' Phenomenon." *Ms.* September 1982: 14–16.

Freud, Sigmund. "On Narcissism: An Introduction." *General Psychoanalytic Theory,* ed. Philip Rieff. New York: Collier, 1976. 56–82.

Friedan, Betty. *The Feminine Mystique.* New York: Norton, 1963.

Friedl, Ernestine. "The Position of Women: Appearance and Reality." *Anthropological Quarterly* 40 (1967): 97–105.

Gallagher, Catherine. "More About 'Medusa's Head'." *Representations* 4 (Fall 1983): 55–72.

Gallop, Jane. "The Immoral Teachers." *Yale French Studies* 63 (1982): 117–28.

Gilbert, Sandra and Susan Gubar. *The Madwoman in the Attic: The Woman Writer and the Nineteenth Century Literary Imagination.* New Haven: Yale University Press, 1979.

Gilder, George. *Sexual Suicide.* New York: Quadrangle Books, 1973.

Gilligan, Carol. *In a Different Voice: Psychological Theory and Women's Development.* Cambridge, Mass.: Harvard University Press, 1982.

Girard, René. "Narcissism: The Freudian Myth Demythified by Proust." In *Psychoanalysis, Creativity, and Literature,* ed. Alan Roland. New York: Columbia University Press, 1978. 292–311.

Greenburg, Dan. *What Do Women Want?* New York: Pocket Books, 1982.

Greer, Germaine. *Sex and Destiny.* New York: Harper and Row, 1984.

Hareven, Tamara K. "Family Time and Historical Time." *Daedalus* 106 (Spring 1977): 57–70.

Hartmann, Heidi. "The Family as the Locus of Gender, Class, and Political Struggle: The Example of Housework." *Signs* 6 (Spring 1981): 366–94.

Heath, Stephen. *The Sexual Fix.* London: The Macmillan Press, Ltd., 1982.

Hertz, Neil. "Medusa's Head: Male Hysteria Under Political Pressure." *Representations* 4 (Fall 1983): 27–54.

Hochschild, Arlie. "Illich: The Ideologue in Scientist's Clothing." *Feminist Issues* 3 (Spring 1983): 6–11.

Illich, Ivan. *Gender*. New York: Pantheon Books, 1982.

Illich, Ivan. *Shadow Work*. Boston: Marion Boyars, 1981.

Irigaray, Luce. *This Sex Which Is Not One*. Trans. Catherine Porter with Carolyn Burke. Ithaca, N.Y.: Cornell University Press, 1985.

Irigaray, Luce. *Speculum of the Other Woman*. Trans. Gillian C. Gill. Ithaca, N.Y.: Cornell University Press, 1985.

Irving, John. *The World According to Garp*. New York: Pocket Books and Simon & Schuster, 1979.

Janeway, Elizabeth. "Woman's Literature." In *Harvard Guide to Contemporary American Writing*, ed. Daniel Hoffman. Cambridge, Mass.: Belknap Press, 1979.

Jones, Ernest. *The Problem of Hamlet and the Oedipus-Complex*. London: Vision, 1947.

Kakutani, Michiko. "Gallery of the Repellent." Review of *Reckless Eyeballing*, by Ishmael Reed. *New York Times*, 5 April 1986: 7:12.

Kleinbaum, Abby Wettan. *The War Against the Amazons*. New York: McGraw-Hill, 1983.

Kolodny, Annette. "A Map for Rereading: or, Gender and the Interpretation of Literary Texts." *New Literary History* 11:3 (Spring 1980): 451–67.

Lacan, Jacques. "The Mirror Stage as Formative of the Function of the I as Revealed in Psychoanalysis." *Ecrits: A Selection*, trans. Alan Sheridan. New York: W.W. Norton & Co., 1977. 1–7.

Lasch, Christopher. *The Culture of Narcissism: American Life in an Age of Diminishing Expectations*. New York: W.W. Norton & Co., 1978.

Lasch, Christopher. "The Politics of Nostalgia." *Harper's Magazine* November 1984: 65–70.

Lasch, Christopher. "Recovering Reality." *Salmagundi* 42 (Summer-Fall 1978): 44–47.

Laslett, Peter and Richard Walls, eds. *Household and Family in Past Time*. New York: Cambridge University Press, 1972.

Laslett, Peter. *The World We Have Lost*. New York: Scribner, 1965.

Leacock, Eleanor. "History, Development, and the Division of Labor by Sex: Implications for Organization." *Signs* 7 (Winter 1981): 474–91.

Lentricchia, Frank. *After the New Criticism*. Chicago: The University of Chicago Press, 1980.

Leonard, John. Review of *Confessions of a Lady Killer* by George Stade. *The New York Times* 26 November 1979: C:18.

Marks, Elaine and Isabelle de Courtivron, eds. *New French Feminisms.* Amherst: The University of Massachusetts Press, 1980.

Martin, Biddy. "Feminism, Criticism, and Foucault." *New German Critique* (Fall 1982): 3–30.

McCracken, Robert. *Fallacies of Women's Liberation.* Boulder, Colorado: Shield's Publishing, Inc. 1972.

Millett, Kate. *Sexual Politics.* New York: Doubleday & Co., Inc., 1970.

Moi, Toril. *Sexual/Textual Politics: Feminist Literary Theory.* London and New York: Methuen, 1985.

Norris, Christopher. *Deconstruction: Theory and Practice.* London and New York: Methuen, 1982.

Poster, Mark. *Critical Theory of the Family.* New York: The Seabury Press, 1980.

Reed, Ishmael. *Reckless Eyeballing.* New York: St. Martin's Press, 1986.

Register, Cheri. "American Feminist Literary Criticism: A Bibliographical Introduction." In *Feminist Literary Criticism,* ed. Josephine Donovan. Lexington: University Press of Kentucky, 1975, 1–28.

Rose, Jacqueline. "Introduction—II." *Feminine Sexuality: Jacques Lacan and the école freudienne,* eds. Juliet Mitchell and Jacqueline Rose; trans. Jacqueline Rose. New York: W.W. Norton & Co., 1982. 27–57.

Sadoff, Dianne F. *Monsters of Affection: Dickens, Eliot, and Brontë on Fatherhood.* Baltimore: The Johns Hopkins University Press, 1982.

Said, Edward. *Beginnings: Intention and Method.* New York: Basic Books, Inc., 1975.

Shechner, Mark. "Male Chauvinist Romp." *The New York Times Book Review* 18 November 1979: 15+.

Showalter, Elaine. "Toward a Feminist Poetics." *The New Feminist Criticism: Essays on Women, Literature and Theory,* ed. Elaine Showalter. New York; Pantheon Books, 1985, 125–43.

Siegel, Fred. "The Agony of Christopher Lasch." *Reviews in American History.* September 1980: 285–95.

Solanis, Valerie. "S.C.U.M. Manifesto." *Sisterhood is Powerful.* Comp. Robin Morgan. New York: Vintage, 1970. 577–83.

Stacey, Judith. "The New Conservative Feminism." *Feminist Studies* 3 (Fall, 1983), 559–83.

Stade, George. *Confessions of a Lady-Killer.* New York: Norton, 1979.

Stade, George. "Romantic Anxiety." *Partisan Review* 40 (1973): 494–500.

Stade, George. "Mailer and Miller." *Partisan Review* 44 (1977): 616–24.

Steinfels, Peter. *The Neo-conservatives: The Men Who Are Changing America.* New York: Simon & Schuster, 1979.

Theriot, Nancy. *Nostalgia on the Right: Historical Roots of the Idealized Family.* Midwest Research Monograph Series: I. Chicago: Midwest Research, Inc., 1983.

Tompkins, Jane P. "Sentimental Power: *Uncle Tom's Cabin* and the Politics of Literary History." *Glyph* 8 (1981): 79–102.

Vance, Eugene. "Love's Concordance: The Poetics of Desire and the Joy of the Text." *Diacritics* 5 (Spring 1975): 40–52.

Watkins, Mel. "Sexism, Racism and Black Women Writers." *New York Times Book Review* 15 June 1986: 1: 35–37.

Westbrook, Robert. "Good-bye to All That: Aileen Kraditor and Radical History." *Radical History Review* 28–30 (1984): 69–89.

Index